DEATH
and
NEUROSIS

DEATH
and
NEUROSIS

Joachim E. Meyer

translated by
Margarete Nunberg

INTERNATIONAL UNIVERSITIES PRESS, INC.
New York

Library of Congress Cataloging in Publication
Data

Meyer, Joachim Ernst.
    Death and neurosis.

    Bibliography: p.
    1. Death—Psychology. 2. Neuroses. I. Title.
BF789.D4M46   616.8'5   73-19951
ISBN 0-8236-1130-2

Translated from the German with the per-
mission of the Publishing house, Vandenhoeck
and Ruprecht, Göttingen. © Vandenhoeck
and Ruprecht in Göttingen, 1973.

Manufactured in the United States of America

To my wife, Ruth Thwaites Meyer

Foreword

During the two-year interval between the original publication of *Death and Neurosis* and this English-Language edition, I have had to ask myself several questions. Is the current approach to death and dying in Western societies still the same as when I was writing this book? Does the phrase "denial of death," which arose almost automatically in every psychological or sociological discussion of this subject over the last decades, still have validity? Are we not confronted with a radical change—a total swing to the other extreme—particularly in the United States?

Avoidance, suppression, and denial of our mortality seem to have been replaced by a growing fascination with death and dying so long pushed aside with evasions, rationalizations, and euphemisms. What prompts a healthy man of thirty or forty years to sign his "living will"? Does he really know, in the prime of life, how he wants to die when life is ebbing? What is really behind the magic formula "dying with dignity"? And how do we explain the growing enthusiasm with which euthanasia is frankly discussed?

This seemingly altered approach to death is far too recent to allow for even tentative interpretation. It may be that modern man is arriving at a more natural, less anxiety-laden attitude toward his own mortality.

But it may equally be that he has accepted another, but no less distorted, resolution of this problem. Considering the astonishing popularity of the theme, one is reminded of Freud's words: "The wanderer who sings in the dark denies his fears, but his singing does not lighten the darkness."

I am personally indebted to Mrs. Margarete Nunberg, who translated the manuscript, and to Mrs. Natalie Altman, the Editor. Both have extended themselves, not only to reproduce the German text accurately, but also to convey the nuances of my meaning.

J.E.M.

Contents

Preface

Interest in the questions of dying and death is once
again beginning to grow, although the general public
still wishes to hear little about them. In medicine—in
connection with revivification and organ transplants
among other things—studies on dealing with the dying
patient are accumulating. Psychological research is
concentrating on empirical findings having to do
with attitudes to death. Sociology has broached the
topic only reluctantly, first investigating funeral and
mourning rites within the framework of changing
forms of society, and subsequently the concept of
"natural death" as stressed by dialectical materialism.
In the psychoanalytic literature, the discrepancy between extensive studies on anxiety, mourning, and
death wishes, on the one hand, and the scarcity of
remarks on the significance of the fear of death, on the
other, is striking.

In view of this, it has seemed meaningful to make
an attempt, as a psychiatrist, to enlarge the theory of
neuroses by including those aspects having to do with
man's mortality. For it is obvious that dying and death
play an important part in the development and course
of the neuroses—a part that has until now barely been
considered.

An attempt of this sort cannot rest solely on clinical psychopathology and psychodynamics. Relevant theological and philosophical concepts, as well as general attitudes toward dying and death, must also be taken into consideration. The necessity—and opportunity—to view *simultaneously* both individual and social attitudes toward death characterizes the difficulty we have had to face.

There is still another, very different difficulty to hurdle: the theme of death, perhaps more than any other, exercises an influence on language. The pathos to which writers are given when they speak of death can be really stupifying. The numerous maxims, ever quoted anew, also tend to be a hindrance to the development of one's own thoughts.

I first discussed this work with Werner Schwidder in July, 1970, shortly before his death. Several colleagues have taken the trouble to examine the manuscript, each from his own particular viewpoint: A. Auer (Catholic theology), W. Bräutigam (psychoanalysis), H. G. Geyer (Protestant theology), G. Patzig (philosophy), J. Zauner (psychoanalysis), and, above all, H. Müller-Suur (psychopathology). For this, I owe them a great debt of gratitude, as I do those co-workers in the Department with whom I have discussed my study thoroughly. My special thanks go to Mrs. Marianne Kaufhold for her indefatigable work on the manuscript and to Mrs. Erika Gross, the librarian of the Department.

Göttingen, Fall, 1972

Introduction

What questions, worries, fears, affect man in view of dying and death?

We yearn for a quick and painless dying, and yet we do not want to be unprepared when death over-takes us. We know that to die means to die alone. We do not know the hour of our death. We think of death as the termination of every ability to plan and are, therefore, concerned about whether we are in a posi-tion to make proper use of our lifetime. We think of those for whom we will no longer be able to provide. We ask ourselves whether dying is painful—worse, perhaps, than we will be able to endure. We do not know what comes after death. So we think about what will happen to our body and, perhaps, whether there may be a further existence after death (Diggory and Rothman). The following aspects of these problems are particularly prominent in man's thoughts: the time of our death, dying alone, and the "hereafter."

The uncertainty about the hour of one's death has to do, to begin with, with the fear of having to die too soon, before one's time, before one has "finished." Man, as a future-directed, planning creature, is parti-cularly vulnerable to this uncertainty (Bally, 1964). The significance of the *hora incerta* becomes clear

1

when one contrasts the uncertainty about when we
will die with the certainty of the fact of our death.[1]
With regard to other things that may befall us in life,
the certainty that they will occur is never linked with
an almost equal degree of uncertainty about the
"when" of their occurrence. There are, for human
beings, no comparable experiences. Our mortality is
real, and yet it is almost impossible for us to adapt to it
in a "goal-directed" way, since we do not know
whether our life will come to an end this very night or
years hence. "Not for a single moment should you be
confident that life will go on, for time, like a hidden
tiger, lurks in ambush to slay the unsuspecting" (Budd-
hist Scriptures).

Worry over the uncertainty of the length of time
that is still left begins to dwindle the closer we come to
old age—the period of "natural" death. With the
isolation that results from the death of people of the
same age, and with the awareness of biological limits,
the aging person is less subject to the risk inherent in
this uncertainty in terms of time. With advancing age
the fear lest death suddenly interrupt the history of
one's life—that continuum of past, present, and future
—also diminishes. On the significance that the proportion between time lived and time still left for living
has for one's attitude toward life and death, Scheler
(1933) comments, "In seeing, feeling, and experiencing the fact that the difference between life lived and
life still to be lived grows and grows in favor of the life
that has been lived, I see and experience, at the same

[1] "Man's uncertainty about the hour of death is not simply a
gap in biological knowledge, rather it is a nonknowing of one's
own destiny" (Landsberg, 1937, p. 13).

time, an inundation of spiritual acts transcending life which becomes ever more ready for dying. This process occurs in correspondence to the spiritual maturation of the personality" (p. 46).

The problem of *dying alone*, the knowledge that no one is able to accompany us on our way into the unknown, is probably the fact that many, in contemplating dying and death, are most clearly conscious of and most deeply fear. The patient's desire not to be left alone till the last moment and the survivor's obligation (experienced willingly, unwillingly, or uneasily) to see to it, this seems to us self-evident. It implies that every man is aware of this specific characteristic of death, of the agony of being left alone by all his fellow men— even if he himself has never seen a person dying, has never himself been gravely ill. That profound anxieties are linked with the idea of *"seul mourir"* ("dying alone") can also be inferred from the fact that joint suicide[2], in the "love death" of passion, is, more than any other willed death, thought of as a joyous, seductively attractive deliverance.

The idea of the *"hereafter"* is implied as soon as the question is posed of what happens to the individual when he is dying. Is the whole of death completed at that time? Is death the termination of being, or is it the start of another form of existence? Notions of the beyond—aside from their religious contents—have the function of guaranteeing one's existence as a soul or, even more, one's consciousness, beyond death. The terror of death, the difficulty we have in conceiving our *total* death, lies in the fact that this would mean

[2] Heinrich von Kleist's "love-death alliance" is the most impressive example of joint suicide (see Schmidt).

the extinction of consciousness, the termination of psychic existence. If one draws a parallel with sleep (compare the euphemistic terms for dying: "closing one's eyes," "going off to sleep"), one sees that, in the case of sleep, man knows that upon awakening he will resume being conscious, and the question of a "hereafter" does not present itself. With death, on the other hand, there is the irreversibility of the extinction of consciousness. Despite this, the question of the "hereafter" emerges: whether death is actually the radical termination, or whether man's spiritual continuation, something analogous to the consciousness of the living, will still be possible.

Some sleep disturbances bring to mind an (unconscious) parallel to problems surrounding death. Patients with sleep disturbances occasionally seem to be rendered uneasy by the question of whether they are actually going to experience an awakening and a return of consciousness, or whether with their falling asleep, their nonreawakening might possibly already be sealed. This disquietude manifests itself as a resistance to falling asleep.[3]

With the fading of the belief that a beyond exists, survival on earth in terms of a good remembrance, of our children,[4] or through our works has gained increasingly in importance. These mundane substitutes

[3] We meet the same theme in the English child's prayer:
  Now I lay me down to sleep
  I pray the Lord my soul to keep
  If I should die before I wake
  I pray the Lord my soul to take.
[4] "In motherhood, woman is given the wonderful opportunity of directly experiencing the sense of immortality" (Deutsch, 1945, Vol. II, p. 1).

for the doctrine of the immortality of the soul have acquired great significance with regard to questions about the meaning of life and, thereby, for that mastering of the reality of death of which modern man is capable. Or, we can turn the question around and ask, with Money-Kyrle, why do we strive so intensely for immortality, for work that will outlast us, for a continuation of life in our children, if there is no fear of death?

Considering what is expected of man in terms of death and his lifelong consciousness of his own mortality, the question inevitably arises of how man is at all capable of living—how, to use Freud's formulation, faced with the fact of death, he can enjoy, love, and work. To make the question even more pointed, does an adequate, "normal" attitude toward death exist at all? Can man ever really accept his mortality? It seems that in our increasingly rationalized world, which is detached from religious ties, fear of life often takes the place of fear of death—for instance, in the form of a feeling of emptiness and meaninglessness (Plessner). On the other hand, Feifel (1959a) emphasizes that, "In gaining an awareness of death, we sharpen and intensify our awareness of life."

For the time being, we shall leave to one side the fact that our relation to death is to a great extent dependent on contemporary history in that it is determined by the influence or the absence of religious ideas about the beyond. We shall likewise ignore the significance of one's age with regard to the attitude toward death. Rather, we shall take as our point of departure, two simple experiences that are familiar to everyone or can be conjured up without effort:

Thinking of death, taking leave of a dying person, passing a cemetery may be frightening experiences, but they may be calming and comforting as well. Insofar as they are frightening, we are reminded of Bacon's remark, "Men fear death, even as children are afraid to go into the dark." Insofar as they are comforting, they can be explained by Seneca's words, "In order never to fear death, I am always thinking of it."

These modes of experience in dealing with death are possible for the reason that man's approach to internal and external experiences can take place basically in two ways that may have opposite consequences. These two modes of approach may be described as *attention* and *concentration*, in terms of the psychology of perception as *"attention volontaire"* and as *"attitude spectaculaire passive"* (Leroy).[5] (Compare, also Straus, 1949.) In the first case, it is a question of an actively observing, vigilant, anxiously concerned attitude in which the individual is prepared for anything, and his reaction to whatever may happen to him is, as it were, always held in readiness. "Attitude spectaculaire" on the other hand, means keeping oneself open for what will be forthcoming, for future experiences from within or without. With this attitude, I do not look around in tense readiness for action, "keeping my ear cocked" and "feeling out" what may come; instead, I let my eye rest on things and give myself up to my world, looking, listening, and sensing.

These polar modes of approach probably do not,

[5] "Concentration" or *attitude spectaculaire passive* corresponds to receptive attention, whereas "attention" or *attention volontaire* is more active in nature.

under normal conditions, occur as strict alternatives, but are always intermingled. It is, however, only if the concentrative attitude prevails that a full perception of the world, not constricted by fear and apprehension, can be achieved; it takes in my body, my course of life, my relations with others. Out of this posture alone am I able to accept what is given, what is possible, and what is in the offing; and—this is not passivity per se—to adapt myself to perceiving signals of danger without distortion and to react to them appropriately. Out of this posture alone can I, on the other hand, recognize possibilities and capacities for spontaneous action of my own—*Konzentrative Entspannungsüb-ungen* (Meyer, 1961b). This, however, is generally valid: the specific kind of approach determines whether the perception of my bodily functions either makes me a hypochondriac or allows me to manage in accordance with my strength; whether intercourse with other people leads to disappointment and distrust, or to relationships in which I accept as my equal the other one with his demands and his vagaries.

From this differentiation of the modes of approach, we can see why becoming aware of the fact that we are mortal can cause anxiety, and why, on the other hand, this awareness can dissolve anxiety so that we are able to familiarize ourselves with death.

Muensterberger (1963) has described one aspect of this process: "With life in the center of attention, death is implicitly evaded. On the other hand, hunger, sterility, loneliness, or illness are experienced as permanent harbingers of the inescapable bad ending inherent in all life" (p. 171). At this point one may go back to Sartre's alternative (*attendre la mort*—wait for death—as against *s'attendre à la mort*—prepare ourselves for it); the anxiously concerned attitude, continuously reckoning with all possible threats, corresponds to that waiting for death with which man— if he is fully aware of it—cannot in the long run live. It is only being prepared for death that allows us to associate with the world and with people and to distinguish between genuine and alleged dangers.

Fear of Death as a Determinant in the Origin of Neuroses

> *"It is ultimately the fear of death which is behind our cravings to acquire, possess, and incorporate, behind our greed and sadism and the predatory aspects of our modes of life"* [*Riviere, 1932*].

From these two modes of turning toward the world (attention and concentration) and the two corresponding attitudes toward death, consequences follow for the interpretation of the origin of neuroses. For, if the "attentive" attitude prevails and anxious tension further increases, mechanisms of compensation have to be mobilized in order to maintain the dynamics of the process of living. Accordingly, we believe that we can demonstrate that:

1. the fear of death is of determining significance for the *genesis* of many neuroses;

2. the absence of neuroses that make their appearance *for the first time* in old age is to be traced above all to the increasing realization of inevitable, impending death;

3. fear of death is not a derivative of other anxieties, but has to be understood as a *basic* process. Separation anxiety, castration fear, and guilt may be

9

derived from it and may be interpreted as equivalents of the fear of death, explainable in terms of life history.

Before trying to demonstrate these ideas, however, we wish to deal with some possible objections that might be raised against this hypothesis.

First is the *self-contradictory character of the death experience*, the impossibility of experiencing one's own death. We encounter this idea over and over again in the theological, philosophical, and psychoanalytic literature of past and present. Although everyone is aware that biological death implies the end of consciousness, of the soul, of the self, this fact of man's mortality is opposed by the fact that we ourselves cannot actually conceive of our no longer existing. "Hence the psycho-analytic school could venture on the assertion that . . . in the unconscious every one of us is convinced of his own immortality" (Freud, 1915a, p. 289). Thus, the "must" of dying, admitting of no exception, has not become an inner reality. "Were it so, death would be natural to man, a *vérité éternelle*, and not a *factum brutum*" (Plessner, 1951, p. 364).

Edwards (1967) has explained that in order to comprehend another's death it is necessary that the one who is comprehending survive as a spectator. In imagining my own death, on the other hand, I myself disappear as an observer. What makes the thought of my own death so disquieting is precisely the "annihilation of the spectator" and of his world.[1]

At first glance one might conclude that it is impossible to come to terms and master the idea of one's own

[1] "The Ego can not imagine itself dead" (Rosenzweig, 1954, p. 18) and "There is no possibility for the thinking ego, in its insight: 'I shall cease to exist,' to think itself away in thinking, that is to

death. It is true that because it is impossible to anticipate the experience of one's own death, confrontation
with it becomes equally impossible, particularly with a
posture determined solely by *attention volontaire*, for
no "strategic" focusing on it is conceivable. Because
the problem of death cannot be mastered if such an
attitude prevails, does not, however, justify not treat-
ing it as a real problem. The point here is, indeed, not
the fact of dying but the experiencing of death (Rosenzweig) as a task, as an opportunity for man that can be
postponed and denied, yet cannot be eliminated as
irrelevant.

It will have to be demonstrated in the following
exposition that it is precisely this character of death as
"absent presence" (as Feifel, 1959a, has termed it) that
makes it extremely difficult for us to cope adequately
with our mortality. The *factum brutum* consists in the
very fact that it is impossible for me to focus on a
certainty of the "how" of *my* death.

Death Does Not Exist in the Unconscious

Freud has given expression to this conviction several
times in similar formulations:

> What we call our 'unconscious'—the deepest
> strata of our minds, made up of instinctual im-
> pulses—knows nothing that is negative, and no
> negation; in it contradictories coincide. For that
> reason it does not know its own death, for to that
> we can give only a negative content. Thus there is

---

say, vividly to experience this insight" (Gehlen, 1962, p. 309).

"My death cannot be experienced by me. Dying, I suffer
death, but never do I experience it" (Jaspers, 1965, p. 220).

nothing instinctual in us which responds to a belief
in death [1915a, p. 296].

The high-sounding phrase, 'every fear is ulti-
mately the fear of death', has hardly any meaning,
and at any rate cannot be justified. It seems to me,
on the contrary, perfectly correct to distinguish
the fear of death from dread of an object (realistic
anxiety) and from neurotic libidinal anxiety. It
presents a difficult problem to psycho-analysis, for
death is an abstract concept with a negative content for which no unconscious correlative can be
found [1923, pp. 57-58].

But the unconscious seems to contain nothing
that could give any content to our concept of the
annihilation of life . . . nothing resembling death
can ever have been experienced; or if it has, as in
fainting, it has left no observable traces behind
[1926, p. 130].

But this means: An unconscious that contains
nothing that is negative does not admit of the assump-
tion of a *neurotic* fear of death because it is inconceivable that a neurosis should arise without there being a
conflict with contents of the unconscious. We shall
have to deal thoroughly with this view, particularly by
referring to the work of Melanie Klein and, from a
more empirical viewpoint, to the section on death
dreams.

Fear of Death Is Realistic Anxiety

If death is certain for *all* human beings and if, in
addition, it cannot be anticipated as a personal experi-

ence, no fundamental psychodynamic significance can be attributed to the fear of death; the fear of death has, on the contrary, to be regarded as an epiphenomenon which is to be traced back to other contents of the unconscious (see Hoffman and Brody; Rheingold; Slater). Therefore, fear of death cannot be neurotic anxiety, but always has to be realistic anxiety.

Can any general statements be made about the degree to which fear of dying and death are *realistic anxieties*, or merely an internal anxiety that has been transformed into seemingly realistic anxieties? That realistic anxieties can in fact play an important part in the fear of dying and death becomes immediately evident when close relatives (or oneself) are stricken by a severe illness. This anxiety has, to begin with, entirely the character of a biologically meaningful signal, comparable to pain; for it mobilizes all the forces and possibilities of fighting the illness and of strengthening the powers of defense and of life. If we stay with this example, we see, however, that an event of this sort can also at the same time mobilize (beyond the realistic anxiety for the patient and his illness) the anxieties that belong to deeper strata.[2] This becomes most obvious in the especially vehement reactions that are evoked in us by life-threatening illnesses of children and young people, for they come upon us unexpectedly and thus often prevent us from mentally preparing ourselves for them. In his study on the guilt reaction of parents whose children are sick, Gardner comes to the con-

[2] "It is questionable whether there is any such thing as a normal fear of death; actually the idea of one's own death is subjectively inconceivable, and therefore probably every fear of death covers other unconscious ideas" (Fenichel, 1945, p. 208).

clusion that this reaction is the manifestation of a
mechanism of defense, and of the development of
sensitivity in the face of the threat to one's own
existence inherent in the illness as such.

Actually, illness and dying of those who are our
own age should hit us harder; because the biological
phases of life are comparable, we should experience
that much rather as a *memento mori*. The knowledge
that as mortal men we have a common destiny seems,
however, to alleviate in some measure our personal
burden. (See von Gebsattel, 1954; Weisman and
Hackett.)

Apart from great catastrophes or special situations
of direct encounter with dying and death, realistic
anxieties play only a minor role in the attitude to
death. Our realistic anxieties, corresponding to our
systems of value, have to do with accident, illness,
hunger, and contempt. Behind these stand basic fears
that are inescapable. Riemann (1969) names the following: fear of giving oneself, felt as ego loss and
dependence; fear of becoming a self, felt as being
unprotected and isolated; fear of change, experienced
as a symbol of one's mortality and insecurity; fear of
compelling necessity, experienced as finality and lack
of freedom. In labeling these fears—and not only from
the standpoint of experiencing them—the mortality of
man, especially in the case of both the last-named
fears, is touched upon directly; nevertheless, the problem of the relation between these basic fears and the
fear of death remains unexamined. Riemann does,
however, comment in a preceding study (1967) that
man is probably particularly vulnerable to anxiety for
the reason that he is *conscious* of his mortal and tran-

sitory nature. Riemann suggests that man expresses his fear of his own transitoriness by his wish that time stand still.[3]

In Freud's view, the stress with respect to the relation between external dangers and internal ones lies entirely on anxieties aroused by internal dangers, for he states (1926) that "the external danger must also have managed to become internalized if it is to be significant for the ego" (p. 168). These "internal" anxieties make their appearance as general anxiousness (in anxiety neurosis) or as a fear of concrete notions and situations (phobia)—that is to say, as a pseudo-realistic anxiety. Melanie Klein, on the other hand, stresses (1948) that there is no sharp boundary line between realistic anxiety and neurotic anxiety; rather, an interdependence exists between the two, which—more or less marked—can be observed throughout life: external dangers are experienced in the light of internal dangers and are intensified thereby. Every danger that threatens from without, however, in its turn also reinforces internal danger situations. This interdependence, a constituent factor in every neurotic development, creates a vicious circle.

This conception of the continuous interactions of external and internal dangers might contribute to rendering more fruitful the discussion of the genetic factors and those that are merely releasing factors in the development of neuroses—a discussion often carried on only in the alternative sense. In regard to our

[3] "This morning it occurred to me for the first time that my body, this faithful companion, this friend more intimately known to me than my soul, is after all only a sly monster that will end by devouring its master" (Yourcenar, 1951).

topic, this becomes clear if we call to mind those life situations in which the problem of death sometimes suddenly emerges as one of immediate import.

There are, to begin with, the quite objective experiences of aging, of loneliness, of falling ill, and of being ill, as well as the illness or death of people close to the subject. Less threatening but nevertheless likely to permit the emergence of thoughts of death are the following situations: failing when one is confronted with a specific task and neglecting to do what one feels to be one's duty. Paradoxically, after a task has been completed or a goal has been reached, or one has been given the highest office to which one could have aspired, thoughts of death emerge. It is precisely during periods of achievement, of success, or when engaged in an activity that is directed entirely toward the future that this fear may make itself felt. It is, in this case, felt as untimely, irrational, and hence is particularly frightening. Freud (1916) calls it "being wrecked by success." Finally, our knowledge—always present after childhood—that death may appear at any time is capable of becoming an overpowering fear, even if we are not exposed to any external threat.

Death Dreams

If we are right in assuming that the mortality of man plays a role in the genesis of many neuroses, then the subject of death in undisguised or in censored form must be found in dreams too. According to Freud (1913b), dumbness, pallor, being undiscoverable, are common representations of death in dreams.

A few examples:

A hypochondriac patient about whom Bräutigam reported (1956) dreamed:

> I am half below and half above ground, one leg is inside and the other outside. I am looking for my grave under the ground. Someone from above asks: what are you looking for there? I say: it is better to look for one's grave in good time [p. 412].

The grave theme clearly expresses itself in a similar way in the following dream:

> I am deep down in a hollow; I am trying to climb upward and have already reached the edge, which I hold onto with my hands; someone comes and steps on my hands. I have to let go and fall back into the hollow [Fromm, 1951, p. 18].

Both the following dreams characterize the situa-

tion of a person who believes that through his own
action he has got into deathly—now no longer avoidable—danger:

> I am walking on a narrow strip of land toward
> a swamp. It is quite dark; I cannot see my way.
> It seems to me that I am completely lost and have
> the feeling: if I go one step further, I shall lose my
> footing and drown [Fromm, 1951, p. 180].

> I am sitting in a bathtub, which is filled al-
> most to the brim. When I move a bit, the surface
> of the water starts swinging and the water laps
> heavily over the brim. To stop that, I make coun-
> termovements, but the billowing becomes ever
> stronger and I can no longer control it. Then I
> appear no longer to be in the bathtub, but am
> drifting on an enormous ocean surface, helplessly
> at the mercy of the waves which have now become
> high as a house [Kemper, 1955, p. 140].

The examples presented here as death dreams do
admit, of course, of other interpretations, such as have
been given by the authors. Kemper, for instance,
interpreted the bathtub dream of his depressive obsessional neurotic patient as a contest between his ego
and the unleashed components of his id. Fromm points
to the desperate circumstances of the dreamer's life,
which, like the dream, make it possible to understand
her repeated suicide attempts. Interpretations such as
these are by no means mutually exclusive; on the
contrary, the emotional experience of fear and danger
is in each instance analyzed on a different level. The
dream interpretations given by the writers throw light
on the therapeutically important questions: from what

direction and in what situation had the individual felt himself threatened, and why does he feel so at the present time? The character of deathly danger emphasized here shows, on the other hand, that in the sufferer's inner experience and feeling, it is a question not only of weaknesses or defects, of failing or erring, but of life and death. This is not to say that the dreamers are caught in a particularly severe neurosis —that is, in an existential crisis; for a single dream taken by itself does not allow us to draw conclusions with reference to the total state of the psyche.

The following dream demonstrates that the death theme can be expressed pictorially in even more direct terms:

> I come home and unlock the door to my apartment. As I enter, I have a feeling that somebody is there. First I look down the corridor, then into the kitchen. Nobody is there. Then I look in my room, and an old man is there. He is over sixty (I have seen him several times before on the street-car), and he looks like Death. He has entered as a burglar. Frightened, I run out of the apartment. But I cannot lock the door from the outside, and I ring at my neighbor's apartment and call for help. But no one shows up and no one opens the door for me. I am totally alone, and then I go back into my apartment where the sinister one is, into my room [Herzog, 1960, p. 229].

Herzog comments on this: death has pushed his way into us and can be locked neither in nor out. We have to deal with him by ourselves, without any help from others.

We must now ask about the meaning to be attributed to those dreams that deal with the death of *other*
persons. Are they invariably to be interpreted as *death
wishes*? The psychoanalytic theory of death wishes is
based on the fact that our attitude toward those for
whom we feel the greatest love is always ambivalent
and is therefore also one of concealed hate. Freud held
the view that this conflict of ambivalence becomes
acute in the case of death; therefore, highly intense
mourning is necessary for the concealment of hostility,
let alone satisfaction over the death: "A hostile current
of feeling such as this against a person's nearest and
dearest relatives may remain latent during their lifetime—that is, its existence may not be betrayed to
consciousness either directly or through some substitute. But when the person who is loved and hated at
the same time[1] dies this is no longer possible and the
conflict becomes acute" (1913a, p. 63). Freud gives no
further explanation in "Totem and Taboo" of why the
ambivalence does not lead to conflict during the loved
person's lifetime—or especially during his lifetime—or
why when he dies it cannot be erased, for instance, by
glorification, as happens when old people mourn the
deaths of their contemporaries. There is another explanation for the hostility toward the dead that is
concealed by excessive mourning—a situation that can
no doubt often be observed: the bitterness of the
survivor. The closer the tie was, the more does the one
who is left behind feel forsaken—all the more since it is
no longer possible to make any assertion about the
state and fate of the one who is dead. "Hate toward

---

[1] Strachey has omitted this section of the sentence in his
translation.

the deceased is jealousy no less than feeling of guilt . . .
And when the burden of life reimposes itself upon the
one who is left behind, the situation of the dead one
easily appears to him to be the better condition"
(Horkheimer and Adorno, 1969, p. 255).

Caruso (1968) has drawn a parallel between death
and the separation of lovers. In separation, too, it is
generally the one who remains behind that bears the
heavier burden; it is he who needs consolation, rather
than the one who has gone away. In this connection, it
should be remembered that marital partners who have
been living together for many years or decades quite
often openly express the wish to be allowed to die first.

In the psychoanalytic view, the reason why the
latent hostility for a loved person becomes manifest
when he dies is that the secret death wishes now have
indeed been realized, leaving behind a culprit who is
no longer able to make amends. It will be necessary,
however, to consider the fact that the abrupt ending of
the relations caused by the death of "the other one" is
apt to arouse a feeling of envy at his suddenly leaving
this wearisome world and breaking off, as it were
one-sidedly, friendship and love. From this it follows
that the words spoken at the burial service are intended to comfort the living, rather than to express
anxiety over the uncertain fate of the deceased. In this
light, dreams of the death of loved ones appear as
encoded forms of the fear of death.

It should also be borne in mind that a change has
taken place in the hitherto general acceptance of the
hypothesis that there is a radical distinction between
the *manifest* dream content and the *latent* one. Erikson (1954), in his study, "The Dream Specimen of Psy-

choanalysis," has shown for the first time in detail that the latent infantile wish that provides the energy for the reawakened conflict, and thereby also for the dream, is imbedded in a manifest dream structure which "on every level reflects significant trends of the dreamer's total situation" (p. 55). This is an important point in relation to our concept; for it follows that death dreams such as those we have given here— examples taken from various case histories and interpreted along our own lines—do more than merely reveal the general theme of anxiety and threat; they signalize the dreamer's unsuccessful attempt to cope with death. The immediate symptoms may express the attitude toward death only in the coded form of particular fears for physical well-being and the functioning of organs, just as is the case with the hypochondriac.

It would not be difficult, by intensively exploring dreams of neurotic patients, to collect further proofs for Melanie Klein's view that the fear of death is found in the unconscious. During the course of struggling with Freud's theory of the death instinct, Klein (1948, 1955), arrived at the view that the "fear of annihilation" is encountered as a response to the death instinct in the deepest strata of the psyche. "Since the struggle between the life and death instincts persists throughout life, this source of anxiety is never eliminated and enters as a perpetual factor into all anxiety situations" (Klein, 1948, p. 116).[2] Anxiety has its origin in the fear of death.

---

[2] Grotjahn (1951) offers some good examples of death dreams. He writes, "It seems that the unconscious knows the wish to kill and the fear to die in the form of mutilation fear" (p. 418).

Anxiety at Different
Phases of Life

Freud's theories of anxiety are the point of departure for our next consideration. His first theory of anxiety (1917) says that anxiety arises by way of repressed libido—that is, the repression corresponds to an attempt by the ego at flight from the libido, which is felt as a danger. The affect linked with the repressed idea is transformed into anxiety in the sense of a discharge and a projection of the libido outward, as, for instance, in pangs of conscience. As early as at this point, by the way, Freud distinguishes between realistic anxiety as a manifestation of the instinct of self-preservation, and neurotic, free-floating, anticipatory anxiety. Children who have not yet become acquainted with dangers are without anxiety; in this sense, anxiety is, according to Freud, a product of upbringing.

In "Inhibitions, Symptoms and Anxiety," Freud (1926) rejects his first theory of anxiety; he now makes anxiety the cause of repression, thus adopting a reverse position. Herewith the ego becomes the seat of anxiety. The ego's attitude of anxiety becomes realistic for the first time with the separation from the mother; then—

prepared by repeated object losses—this anxiety changes to castration anxiety. To Freud (1923), fear of death is a development of the fear of castration.

The *second* theory of anxiety unfolds fully in the "New Introductory Lectures" (1933), with the distinction between anxiety as a consequence or expression of a failing of the pleasure principle, and anxiety as a biologically meaningful signal. One can further structurally differentiate realistic anxiety (fear of the external world) from neurotic anxiety (fear of the id) and moral anxiety (fear of the superego).

Against the background of these theories of anxiety, we shall now have to examine how far the various forms of anxiety can be assigned to different phases of life and what relations to the fear of death thereby become discernible. To this point Freud writes: "It must be, therefore, that certain determinants of anxiety are relinquished and certain danger-situations lose their significance as the individual becomes more mature. Moreover, some of these danger-situations manage to survive into later times by modifying their determinants of anxiety so as to bring them up to date" (1926, p. 179).

Bowlby observed *separation anxiety* in hospitalized children between the fifteenth and thirtieth month of life in those instances where children had previously had an undisturbed relation with their mothers; by contrast, he did not observe separation anxiety in those children who had by this age already been seriously harmed in this respect. Separation anxiety thus takes place before the time when fears of death can be observed in children, and especially in those who are

disturbed in their development. Separation anxiety
manifests itself only until the child has become accustomed to the daily but merely transitory separations
from his mother and has learned to be confident of her
return. Separation anxiety is characteristic of the
primary experience of ego and external object; it is
biologically meaningful, since the child at the time is
not capable of living without maternal care; psychologically, it signifies the first stage of an ego experience
and, therefore, the beginning of all individuality.

In separation anxiety, it is the danger of the
separation from the mother that is signalled to the
infant. *Castration fear* results from experiencing a
father who is no longer merely protecting but also
extremely powerful, and whose ties to the mother
prevail over the infant's wishes. What is at stake in this
second phase of anxiety, according to psychoanalytic
theory, is actually the first confrontation with a person
of the same sex. Boys as well as girls are rivals of father
or mother in this phase of development, and the
contest generates an anxiety which—in the male, in
any case—is castration fear. In boys and girls, this
"rival" attitude brings about the "loss" of the mother
who up to then simply belonged to the child's life. The
child loses, one might say, the mother's unrestricted
availability. From this one may conclude that castration fear at the end of the oedipal phase represents a
second stage of the fear of separation from the mother.
In the boy, fear of castration is experienced as fear
concerning the loss of his male identity. In this sense,
castration fear is, *pars pro toto*, fear of death. "The
loss of the genital would mean the end of the creative

power, which preserves and continues life" (Klein, 1948, p. 117; see also, Chadwick).[1]

At this point, it seems necessary to introduce another special form of anxiety, which is biographically and psychodynamically significant, and which is generally—we think—classed with castration fear: the *fear of love*. This is a fear of and during sexual union, which arises from experiences such as the disappearance of ego boundaries at the moment of climax. It would go beyond the context of our deliberations to discuss this problem any further here. Yet, with regard to our topic, it is important to attach significance to this fear of love, especially as an early experience of the adolescent. In so doing, we are aware of the fact that, despite the abundance of references to the relations between love and death in cultural anthropology, the history of religion, and psychology, we have few empirical observations and detailed considerations at our disposal. From the Middle Ages to the present, we encounter the theme of anxiety relating to love in the motif of death dances and of the "Death and the maiden" (on the latter, cf., above all, Edvard Munch's graphic work). Three engravings by H. S. Behaim exist that are especially interesting with regard to these questions: a sheet "Death and the maiden," a repre-

---

[1] In an experimental investigation of young students, Sarnoff and Corwin, with the aid of tests intended to examine castration anxiety, fear of death, and moral attitudes, studied the relations between fear of death and sexual excitement. They found that— quite independently of moral norms—subjects with severe castration anxiety showed a stronger fear of death under visual sexual stimulation than did those with less castration anxiety. The authors stress that their results do not allow any statements on the origin of castration anxiety, but that they do demonstrate its dependence on sexual excitement.

sentation of death with apple and serpent between Adam and Eve; furthermore, from the year 1529, an unusual scene in which man and woman touch each other sexually; while the man pushes a little boy aside, at the same time, death approaches the couple from behind. Inscription: *Mors ultima linea rerum.*[2]

It is striking that terms referring to dying and death are often used as metaphors in the erotic and sexual sphere. Riviere (1932), for instance, quoted verses attributed to John Donne (1573-1631), in which the poet describes his feelings while his beloved is far away: "Absence is presence. Time doth tarry." What is said here about love applies precisely to our attitude to death: it is absent and present at the same time. So long as death is not imminent, our relation to it is timeless. The relations between love and death stand out in the Baroque and particularly in Romanticism. Schlegel (quoted in Rehm, 1928, p. 393) tells us, "Sensual pleasure becomes most evident when it reaches the stage of turning into foreboding of death, and so does death when it turns into lust .... The mystical synthesis of individuals in love consists in their dying together; this is the secret of death."

Life and death become central motifs in youth, as is clearly shown by the frequency with which young people attempt to commit suicide. The experience of being forsaken, of a loss of love, may easily cause the adolescent to step across the boundary of the will to survive. Here again, we refer to Caruso's (1968) study on the separation of lovers, in which, under the motto *"partir c'est mourir un peu,"* he speaks of the deadly

---

[2] I am indebted for this reference to Dr. H. M. Rotenmund, Göttingen.

forlornness of lovers who are separated. The core of
the relation between love and death in youth, however, in all probability lies deeper. As far as we can
see, what is at the bottom is the feeling that the
abandonment to the union of love threatens the individuality that, in adolescence, has only just been fully
attained.[3]

Fenichel and other psychoanalysts have referred to
the similarity between experiences of orgasm and of
dying. As Eissler says, "It is my impression that at the
height of true orgasm . . . a person is ready to surren-
der to death without a struggle" (1955, p. 76). The
emergence of the fear of death is linked partly with the
change in the bodily state brought on by orgasm,
partly with a dissolution of ego boundaries, and partly
with the fact that the relaxation following orgasm may
be experienced as ego loss. "Every type of excitement
tends toward ultimate relaxation. In cases in which the
achievement of such relaxation is regarded as the
terrible sensation of loss of one's ego, it may be
identified with 'death', and on occasions when other
persons would hope for sexual excitement, death may
be feared" (Fenichel, 1945, p. 209). (See also Keiser;
Wyss. The latter speaks of an "ecstatic identity of life
and death in orgasm.") Under a broader aspect, Stekel
(1922) has formulated it thus: "Anxiety, the fear of
annihilation, and the sexual drive, i.e., the longing for
creation, cannot be separated. Both make their appearance in company of the death instinct" (p. 367).

---

[3] "And the death-instinct may culminate in an act that is called
suicide, but actually represents the last sexual act, the last
expression of an instinct that equally comprises death and life"
(Stekel, 1922, p. 367).

Beyme's depth-psychological investigations of frigid
women (1963-1964) point in a similar direction. One
may, perhaps, move a step further in understanding
the fear of love, with the supposition that the act of the
union of love may be experienced at one and the same
time as a reaching of a new phase of life, as a
transformation from which there is no way back, and
as an assent to a life order that includes death.

In moral anxiety, the menacing father is replaced,
as Freud (1923) has said, by the ethical norms of
society, internalized as conscience in the superego. In
many respects, these norms still permit us to recognize
their origin in ideas of the beyond, such as death as
retribution for sin, or the Last Judgment. To these
correspond, in secularized modern times, the world-
immanent ideals that have to do with nations or
society. Under their protection and with their help,
collective and individual fears of death can be soothed.
"National Socialism, for instance, as ideology, was an
anxiety product of this sort. Under the protection of its
mythology, both the collective historical fear of death
and simultaneously the individual fear of death, as
fear of a life that has become meaningless, could be
banished. If the individual is nothing and the nation is
everything . . . the real continuation of the individual's
life in his people guarantees the fulfillment of his
existence . . . ." (Plessner, 1951, p. 352). Tillich, too,
has emphasized that: "It has been observed that fear
of death increases with advancing individualization,
and that people in collectivistic cultures are less subject
to this type of anxiety" (1969, p. 40). Whether in terms
of the beyond or in terms of the continuance of life
through the community, the significance of the ethical

norm in man's attitude to his finiteness is quite
evident.

The theory of separation anxiety in the infant, of
castration fear in the older child, and of moral anxiety
in adolescence and adulthood, gives an initial impression of being a strange network of seemingly banal
observations and a construction entirely oriented to
the beginning of life. The danger of oversimplifying
the concept of man's anxieties can be demonstrated by
an example from Helene Deutsch's otherwise important work (1945): "While in man the fear of castration
is at the center of all anxieties, woman's anxiety is
gradually transformed from the genital fear to the fear
of defloration and rape into the fear of childbirth or
death" (p. 303). We believe, however, that these
anxieties can be shown to represent developmental,
quasi-phase-specific manifestations of the fear of
death. Separation anxiety is, in this sense, an expression of a preconscious, biologically meaningful feeling
of being vitally threatened. Castration fear is the
anxiety that the individual experiences in his search for
independence and for his own creativity. In fear of
love, it is the fear of the loss of one's individuality in
sexual union that manifests itself and perhaps also the
experience of an irrevocably new phase of life. The
moral fear, finally, is closely tied to the question of the
"hereafter." These changing forms of the fear of death
are clearly in evidence only in those instances where
the fear could not be successfully mastered or inte-
grated, or in which its overcoming has been delayed.

The Neuroses

The following more clinically oriented remarks cannot lay claim to completeness. Rather, they represent an attempt to show the process of neurotic repression and encoding of fear of death. In making this attempt, we are aware of the risk of hastily inferring from the more or less obvious, or even prominent, presence of the death motif in some forms of neurosis—its significance for the *genesis* of neurotic developments. Since there is at present, however, no psychoanalytic therapy that directs its attention specifically to the attitude toward dying and death, we are dependent on the study of adult neurotic patients. We shall thus probably not, or only by way of exception, encounter the process of the genesis of neurosis, which takes place in childhood or in early adolescence; rather, in most instances, we shall come upon later developments, which we shall interpret as recapitulations of the primordial dealing with death.

The examples taken from individual forms of neurosis are to illustrate how, in correlation with those aspects of death that in an individual's mind are most strongly cathected with anxiety, various—though by no means specific—symptom formations can come about and symptom shifts may occur. Among these is, first, the transformation of the fear of death into pseudorealistic anxiety, into individual, closely circumscribed fears and partly corresponding defense systems, behind which the threat to life becomes more and more concealed. With the development of neurotic symptomatology, which by means of substitute mechanisms bans the fear of annihilation—that is to say, with his retreat into neurosis—man gains the security of the sick; he can, without being "at fault," withdraw from work and the competitive struggle; this may also be significant with regard to the question of the "hereafter."

Suicide

In addition to neurotic symptom formation, or in its stead, suicide is a way of meeting the fear of death, of mastering it. In these instances, suicide is often preceded for weeks by fantasies in which sometimes the emphasis is on minimizing dying, sometimes on glorifying death as no longer being. The point is *to gain access to death and thus to avoid having to suffer it*.

Suicide may occur instead of neurotic symptom formation if, above all, fear of the emptiness and meaninglessness of life prevails over the fear of dying and death—which applies particularly to adolescents. It may, however, also happen that the neurotic symptom formation culminates in suicide—as, for instance, in anxiety neuroses, some hypochondriases, and neuroses of depersonalization; obviously, this comes to pass when the *anxiety-binding function of the symptom remains insufficient*. It must be added here that not every suicide is necessarily the expression of a neurotically distorted attitude to life and death—for instance, when suicide is preceded by the anticipation of the finiteness of our existence and of the irreversibility of dying, and when killing oneself thus becomes an act of personal decision.

Phobias

We choose phobias as our first example of those neuroses in which the problems of death are psychodynamically significant. If we consider the phobias in the following order of succession: heart phobia, agoraphobia, claustrophobia, animal phobia, fear of the dark, and fear of heights, it becomes evident that in heart phobia the motif of death is experienced as a vital crisis most directly—that is to say, quite consciously—whereas in the other phobias the fear increasingly loses the character of fear of a deadly danger. On the other hand, in about the same order of succession, discernment of the absurd or exaggerated character of such fears increases.[1]

We begin with an example that may be classed with the syndrome of *heart phobia,* even though it shows some traits that are more hypochondriacal than phobic. The patient is a thirty-two-year-old bank employee who has been complaining for a year about a frightening feeling of dizziness and heart sensations:

> The dizziness comes by way of attacks, together with a pressure in the region of the heart,

[1] Feldmann (1967) emphasizes that there is a typical sequence of objects preferred in phobic states.

so that I became afraid of a circulatory collapse.
It never happens while I am lying down; then I am
content and relaxed. When I am sitting, there is a
queer sensation which goes through my whole
body; but when I am walking my trunk starts
twisting as if on springs. If such a thing happens
and my wife is there, she can alert the doctor.
It is good to know there is someone here who can
carry me if need be.

Every day one reads in the papers about cardiac infarction. When my father died from cardiac
infarction—that is just it—then it did not matter
to me. But when Nasser died and with that train
accident which I read about in the paper, it shot
through my body like a hot streak toward the
heart. I am still afraid of dying; I am really too
young for that. If I were to be pulled out of the
family now, when everything has calmed down
with us! There used to be tensions: I had to pass
tests, and there were some financial difficulties.
Now I could have heaven on earth. My professional path, that I know. What I have to expect,
that I know—ninety per cent of it, ten depends on
a higher power. This higher power, that is more
than silly, I cannot understand myself in this.

As a child, the patient suffered from fear of the
dark; he also was afraid of being kidnapped and
dragged away. Concerning the period preceding the
beginning of his illness, when he was a member of the
federal frontier guard, he said, "At that time I was
hard in taking and hard in giving. When I lit a ciga-
rette, I would tell myself: it doesn't matter what makes

you hit the dust." He closed his discourse with the remark, "Throughout my life, I had the feeling of letting something slip by."

Various aspects of the fear of death are implied here: it is not only uncertainty with regard to the hour, not only anxiousness about a sudden, untimely death, but also, and considerably emphasized, the fear of dying alone and helpless. Of special significance is the patient's fear that he might not be allowed to progress on his professional path up to its top, to enjoy a full life. Noteworthy, too, are the details of his states of dizziness, which are closely linked with erect gait and thus, symbolically, with the mastering of the path of his life (see also case, p. 42, below). He has no dizziness when he is lying down; this may be interpreted in the sense of its being a regression to the security of infancy.

What is quite consciously involved in cardiac phobia is the fear—a fear of panic proportions—of heart failure that could occur at any time.[2] The first attack of this sort, today generally termed initial sympaticovasal attack, is the one that as a rule contains most clearly the element of deadly menace. With each repetition, ever stronger early precautionary measures are employed; the actual fear of death recedes in face of the fear of anxiety. The elemental anxiety reaction becomes a phobic one—that is to say, a readiness for perceptions of heart sensations—which is sharpened by anxiety. "With the initial vegetative attack, a new

[2]On the induction of heart phobias through death experiences, see Christian and Hahn and the report published on the previous history and analytical treatment of a patient with a phobic cardiac neurosis (Anon., 1972).

fear enters the life of the heart-phobic patient. . . .
Life takes on the character of a border-situation, as it
were; it is thus being continuously experienced as if
under the breath of Nothingness" (Kulenkampf and
Bauer, 1960, p. 496). Finally, the feeling of anxiety
may fade away to a great extent, while the "neuro-
vegetative" portion dominates the scene (see von Gebsattel, 1959; Kulenkampf and Bauer, 1960; Loeser and
Bry).

The first heart phobic attack often occurs in a
situation in which the patient is about, or is being
forced, to give up a protective relationship of dependence (Bräutigam, 1964; Richter and Beckmann). The
report on the psychoanalytic treatment of a young,
heart hypochondriac shows most instructively the factors of detachment from the mother, together with
ambivalence, death wishes, feelings of guilt and anxiety—the latter in identification with the mother who
has fallen ill—or fear of having to die as retribution.
This ambivalent conflict of separation cannot be traced
back simply to a separation anxiety in childhood that
had been experienced with special intensity. That
conflict is also encountered, as Bräutigam stresses in
this study, in cases in which pampering mothers have
not given children any opportunity to experience and
tolerate the state of being alone. Generally one may
state that early infantile separation anxiety that has
remained unnoticed for decades or has been repressed
in latency erupts with the (delayed) striving to become
independent, directly as fear of death.

Regarding this effort to become independent—and
this means regarding the problems of maturation—the

following statements of a thirty-one-year-old patient suffering from heart phobia are instructive. "I could have achieved so much. What has passed me by, if I die now! I could die and have never had anything to do with a woman. The mad racing of my heart has always pursued me." Here, too, as in the first example, the (oral) motif of a life unlived, of enjoyment of life missed, can be recognized.

The old rule of the more organically sick the patient is, the less psychic reaction, does not apply or no longer seems to do so (at least not so far as patients suffering from cardiac infarction are concerned). This might have to do with the fact that the medical instructions (no smoking, no drinking, rapid weight reduction), given without a discussion of the altered life situation as a whole, are capable of causing an almost intolerable psychic burden in younger infarction patients. The repetition of an infarction may release in them a panic fear that is quite reminiscent in its manifestations of the heart phobia of those who are physically well. Thus, in patients of this sort, it is in the reverse order, as compared with heart phobics, that the feeling of being deadly threatened increases and becomes more prominent with each attack of abnormal cardiac sensations (Kulenkampf and Bauer, 1962).

Agoraphobia shows the heart phobics' annihilation anxiety, only in a watered-down form—namely, as general fear of all the dangers lurking out of doors. "Where anxiety cannot take on its true meaning, it assumes the form of fear and shifts its true meaning into an apprehensive attitude of fear, in which the threats of daily life play an exaggerated, even an immoderate role" (von Gebsattel, 1951, p. 384).

Such homebound persons know very well that their fears "actually" have little or no realistic basis. One of our patients was unable to leave his apartment unless he had first fixed the way he had to go by car according to distances from various medical offices, which he had marked on his city map. For years he had been suffering increasingly from those fears. Only at one period was he free of suffering, for about a year and a half; that was while as a student he belonged to the Berlin SDS—around 1968—and could participate in political activities. Another patient reported almost angrily about his impediment: he could—recently, even when accompanied by his wife—walk or wander about only in areas that offered a view of human habitations, if only on the horizon.

If one asks the patients about the meaning of practices of this sort, they do not as a rule mention that the nearness of physicians or of human beings in general prevents the appearance of anxiety; rather, they say that one needs the comforting feeling of the nearness of people ready to help; yet the patients seem to be quite clear about the fact that in acute danger even physicians are able to give real help only in exceptional cases. It is through these attitudes, typical of the agoraphobic patient, that Freud showed the difference between neurotic and realistic anxiety. The difference lies in the fact that "the danger is an internal instead of an external one and that it is not consciously recognized. In phobias, it is very easy to observe the way in which this internal danger is transformed into an external one—that is to say, how a neurotic anxiety is changed into an apparently realistic one" (1933, p. 84).

The displacing of the problems connected with death becomes even more apparent in *claustrophobia*, that irresistible fear of not being able to get out, of being closed in, which makes its appearance in narrow rooms or closed vehicles. Nowadays, there is rarely a realistically threatening situation that would correspond to this rather frequent phobia. In particular, experiences of being buried under avalanches of stone (e.g., when trenches were bombarded), frequent in wartime, often brought on massive psychogenic reactions.

In *animal phobias*, realistic anxiety, often as a residue from a childhood with overprotective parents, may still be discernible. In most instances, however, it is not the animal that is felt as immediately threatening, but the "animal nature" that is experienced, physiognomically as it were, as disgusting, inhuman in the sense of being incalculable, cruel, or chaotic. It may, however, also happen that the animal represents a person who is felt as threatening. Whether encounter with animals mobilizes instinctual anxieties, whether animal phobias are anxieties of a phylogenetic-archaic or of an ontogenetic-individual nature—these questions cannot be discussed here. It is certain that behind the snakes and spiders of our fairy tales archaic elements are concealed; fear of snakes is common among adults, even though, or perhaps because, they have never actually encountered a snake.

It has often been stressed that children's *fear of the dark* is an equivalent of the fear of death—especially of its (preconscious) early form, the separation fear

(Caprio). In adults, fear of the dark is only rarely quite pronounced. We present below the example that von Gebsattel related in 1954:

> The man in question is a representative of a large trading company; he is energetic, somewhat reckless and egotistic, but competent in practical matters; he is forty-two years old. This man suffered a car accident: a truck hit his car while it was stopping at a street-crossing and threw him against its roof. For a moment everything was dark, but things happened so quickly that he did not even have time to get frightened. He got out quickly, even before his driver, examined the damage, noted down the number of the truck, rode to his office, and resumed his work; but because of headache and incapacity to concentrate, he was unable to continue, either then or the following day.
>
> At first, the patient's situation showed nothing of medical relevance, but on the third day of his stay at the clinic to which the neurologist had sent him, he had a curious symptom to report. He could not step from the lighted hall out into the night without suffering an anxiety attack; he was even unable to enter his dark room unless, facing the brightly lit hallway, he first turned on the light in his room. All this seemed very puzzling to the patient, even humiliating and alarming [p. 407].

In hypnotic treatment, the circumstances of the accident were recapitulated, and during this process the patient experienced the most intense fear of death;

with this he was freed from his symptom. Fear of the dark in adults represents, perhaps, that form of phobia in which the problems of death are farthest removed from consciousness and are most effectively veiled by the fears that are in the foreground.

The phobia most common among adults—and about as frequent as fear of the dark in children—is acrophobia, *fear of heights*. Owing to its specific dependence on the situation of height above a wide, yawning abyss, fear of heights is clinically almost without significance unless it assumes extreme forms and does not allow even looking out of an open window or sitting in a grandstand. Moreover, the person concerned is in most instances capable of observing by himself the relation between his "absurd" fear and the actual circumstances—*the space physiognomy* (Baumeyer; Zutt, 1953).

Loeser and Bry stress the significance, in regard to phobia, of the first experience of death. If it occurs in childhood and is denied by the adults as a reality, or is minimized, a phobia may develop from it— though there may be years during which it is latent, just as with sexual repression. The adult phobia is thus a manifestation of a reactivated infantile fear of death; the well-known precipitating factors (an illness of the subject, death of relatives or acquaintances) are mentioned in this connection. In group therapy, the problems of death are actively broached for the purpose of desensitizing the patients.

Often one will succeed in ferreting out only those events from adult life that, as if they were generating a greater sensitivity, have mobilized fears of death that were subsequently repressed, with resulting symptom formation. The underlying childhood experiences often remain "forgotten." This is also true of the following example, in which the origin of the phobia in childhood may possibly have to do with the patient's relation to his mother—this could not, however, be further clarified. Now, shortly before he was admitted to the clinic, the forty-three-year-old patient had become reconciled with his mother, after having thought for a long time that she had exploited or neglected him in favor of his siblings.

On the symptoms: "I am afraid of stepping into emptiness. I walk as if on cotton. Even while standing I have the urge to hold on to something. While crossing a street I would like to hold on to the streetlamp; it is as if a baby were learning to walk. In bed it is best, but even there I like to place a table before the bed in order not to topple over."

On the formation of the symptom: The dizziness has been present for twelve years. It started when the patient was busy "digging a pit, actually merely a ditch." Suddenly he became afraid of losing his balance. Shortly before this he had been in the hospital for a tonsillectomy. Also in the hospital was a co-worker of his whose leg had had to be amputated following a serious accident during work in the factory. The accident had occurred in connection with a machine that the patient himself had handled the preceding day. His colleague's leg had gotten caught in the machine and was torn off. At the same time, the patient had temporarily had to attend to a gas generator with which he was not familiar, and servicing it has initially made him anxious. It was at this gas generator that the patient had recently, as he stresses, by circumspection and quick action saved the lives of two workmen.

This case makes clear, too, that we may find it difficult or even impossible to determine whether the factors leading to the symptom formation connected with fear of death were "causative" or "precipitating" ones. Should we regard the childhood experiences (in our case unknown) as the decisive pathogenic factor, or should we rather regard them as a factor contributing to the development of a neurotic disposition?

Hypochondriasis

The constant concern for one's physical well-being leads to an abnormal relation to one's body and an entire system of control and safety measures to protect it. Several of the cases Feldmann (1972) has described so excellently in his monograph demonstrate clearly how at the outset the threat is still experienced directly as fear of death; later on, with the development of the peril-reducing practices, the question of dying and death is no longer articulated. Case 4 may serve as an example; the patient's entire concern is finally directed to the exhaustion of his strength: "Six years ago, my state of health was miserable: that is to say, once the ship starts sinking, one wakes up, and so I took notice of it." While previously, he said, he exploited his body, his present concern with his body he calls "a consideration of what has become necessary" (p. 41).

Feldmann's case 1 is noteworthy for the symptom

transformation, which expresses the turning away
from the realm of organs that have been experienced
as menacing. During a training course, the forty-five-
year-old chief building inspector falls ill with heart
trouble and expresses fear of a cardiac infarction.
When, however, his wife dies from a cardiac infarction, his heart troubles and fears more or less abate.
Instead, the disturbances gradually spread to the
head, belly, and legs; the patient now thinks of a brain
tumor, he becomes unsteady on his legs "as if I no
longer had any weight at all, and were just staggering
along."

The first of the two cases Feldmann represents in
detail shows most clearly how the initial situation
("The fear of harboring a deadly illness held me a
prisoner") shifts more and more into a fear of any
burden. ("The disease curve seemed to slide down into
the infinite.") The compulsive pedantry with which
this patient described himself contains self-observation
sharpened to the point of the grotesque, and the corresponding ritual of defense. His description closes
with the following words: "I try to get out of the way
of such things as far as possible in order to be sure that
these symptoms do not appear again. When I elude the
dangers, that cannot be done completely, to be sure;
that I cannot achieve, but I would certainly like to" (p.
106).

With regard to the veiling of the primary experience which in the course of hypochondriacal developments is demonstrable time after time, the following
is still to be mentioned: it is not infrequent that the
condition is precipitated and a tendency to hypochondriasis develops as a result of an illness suffered by

someone close to the patient (especially the mother) or an illness suffered by himself. With a suitable disposition, events of this sort, especially if experienced as unexpected, are obviously apt to shake the naive attitude that can be paraphrased in the words: "Surely, nothing will happen to me." This "pattern of defense" is particularly pronounced in persons of younger or middle age, and it is with corresponding frequency that we encounter phobias and hypochondriases at these ages. "The fear of death is present far more often with the living than with the dying. At the time when a man is strong and mighty, and by the law of averages still far from his estimated end, he seems to fear death most" (Hutschnecker, 1959, p. 248).

Obsessional Neuroses[3]

In his study of the onset of the anancastic syndrome, Skoog (1965) found that in over seventy per cent of the pronounced cases a death motif at the onset was the most frequent "security-disturbing" experience. Earlier Freud (1909) referred to death among relatives or neighbors, in this connection. Here, the death in and of itself is probably feared less than unexpected dying, which is always possible, immanent in life. Skoog mentions a young man who developed breathing difficulties following his father's death and some tragic events about which he, as an employee of a life

[3]Obsessional neuroses and phobias are dealt with separately here, although it is, we think, basically more appropriate to regard them as a psychopathological entity, and to speak only of an anancastic pole and a phobic pole within the obsessional neuroses (Janzarik).

insurance company, had been informed: "One day I shall stop breathing, but when? This year, tomorrow, the next minute?" And he continued, "I must remember to breathe, for breathing is a thing that is absolutely necessary for life.... I must breathe consciously, I hardly dare to fall asleep.... Think if just this breath should be the last one" (1965, p. 31).

In contrast to this close correlation between preoccupation with death and the onset of the anancastic syndrome, a totally different picture is presented in pronounced obsessional neuroses of some duration. Whereas the hypochondriac has developed a "safety system" to safeguard his body, what concerns the obsessional individual is his relations to the outside world, to his contemporaries, to those around him. He is, therefore, compelled incessantly to control everything that happens around him, including his own body functions. The fact that the concern with death —as a fear of being killed, but also of killing—is not completely absorbed by the mechanisms of defense is shown in statistics (Schwidder, 1972) on over a hundred obsessional neurotic and phobic patients who not only reported on feelings of constriction, but a third of whom complained of fear of the dark, and an even somewhat larger number of fear of death.

It is this world stripped of the possibility of simple, natural chance to which the obsessional neurotic in his constant fear of the unexpected has become prey (see von Gebsattel, 1938; Göppert; Meyer, 1957). He seems to be afraid of everything. Tillich (1969) has termed this "fear of fate." These fears overshadow all concrete forms of anxiety and impart to them their ultimate gravity. The emotional impact of such general fear is, as a rule, more direct than that of the fear of death; the element of chance is common to both. "Fate means the reign of chance" (p. 40). With this is linked the obsessional neurotic's incapacity for enjoyment. Friedman (1961) described a patient who was suffering from sleep disturbances and fear of death, and who as a child had suffered from fear of darkness; he was afraid above all that he would be forgotten by his fellow men. This fear was linked with the idea of missing something important, something excitingly new: "Something really new happens only when I'm not around, before my time or after my time, before I was born or after I'm dead."

The accidental, the unanticipated, pose special dangers for the obsessional neurotic: he is ever on the alert for uncleanliness, disorder, infection, or illness; never must he, through neglect or oversight, permit any of those to approach him. In severe (malignant) obsessional neuroses that have not through regression or symbiosis altogether given up their personal struggle with an undependable world, rituals are added to the usual obsessional mechanisms. These serve as magic ceremonials: they ward off evil or undo its effect if it is already present. To the obsessional patient in this state, it is omnipresent death—which is possible at any time and always befalls a person unexpectedly—that constitutes *the* central threat to existence. We are indebted to Skoog (personal communication) for a particularly instructive case:

> The man in question was a forty-year-old aca-demician (principal specialty: philosophy), whose mother was severely hypochondriacal. He grew up in a family of sectarian religious beliefs; during his entire childhood, his religious life was subject to strong fluctuations between ecstatic joy and

apocalyptic terror. Following his adolescence, and more intensely after his twentieth year, he suffered from obsessive thoughts of death; these ideas were so intense and so concrete that sometimes, in his fantasy, he felt he was already dead. When he had to leave his family, and thus also his "habitual existence," he developed agoraphobia. After his mother's death from lung cancer, (he was at that time thirty-two years old), he began to fear that he too had lung cancer because he was a heavy smoker. He was afraid of anaesthesia, in that unconsciousness (to his way of feeling) anticipated death. His fear of death appears on three planes: as a vegetative sensation of annihilation manifested in attacks at night, as agoraphobia, and in the form of obsessive existential pondering over death. These symptoms hardly ever appeared simultaneously, but made their appearance one after the other. When the patient was once suffering from gallstones he forgot the whole problem of death; "My problem had become so primitive, concrete, topical, and localized." His thoughts about death were often linked with the fear lest it might get "too late" for him, so that change would no longer be possible. "Life, to me, is the art of meeting death."

The case is noteworthy, too, in that the vegetative anxiety attacks at night are reminiscent of a heart phobia; in addition, hypochondriases are present, as well as agoraphobia and an existential obsessive pondering over death. The latter did not—as one might perhaps conjecture—constitute a rationalization that

would be at this intellectual patient's disposal at any
time, as it were; it was rather one of the available
forms of obsessional neurotic symptoms, the only one
in which the problem could be comprehended in an
apparently largely uncoded expression. (It should be
added that it is not rare for an obsessional neurotic to
command an amazing—although indeed only rational
—understanding of the meaning of his symptoms.)

In obsessional neuroses, too, one can demonstrate a
symptom transformation, proceeding from the feeling
that one's very existence is being menaced to fears of
matter that is decaying or dead. The following example by Erwin Straus (1938) is a case in point. It
consists of a letter of a woman patient which, because
of its outstanding vividness, will be presented almost
unabridged:

> In November 1918, on the occasion of a birth-
> day celebration, a bouquet of flowers was put on
> the bed. My cousin, who had a cute three-year-
> old boy, removed the bouquet from the bed, with
> the words, "Flowers ought not be put on a bed."
> Three weeks later her child was . . . . From that
> time on I watched very carefully that no more
> flowers were placed on the bed. I am very fond of
> beautiful flowers, but I can no longer touch them
> or have any standing in my apartment. This, how-
> ever, came about only after I had a child myself
> and he was over a year-and-a-half old. I was in
> continuous fear for the child, fear lest he be taken
> from me.
> In January 1931, a very dear, good, and old
> friend, who almost belonged to the family, ...

His wife, who has no other friends or relatives here, came to us every Sunday after having been at the . . . . That did not disturb me in the beginning. After four to six months, however, her gloves made me feel uneasy; somewhat later this became true of her coat, shoes, and so on; I watched out that these things did not come too close to ours. That went on until the lady noticed it and stopped coming to see us because she thought I felt an aversion to her. Since we are living near . . . everybody who goes there makes me feel uneasy, and there are many such people if the summer is a very dry one. It is a true migration. If one of those people were to brush against me, I would have to wash the piece of clothing involved in Persil or benzine. Or, if someone who has been there comes to our apartment, I cannot move properly. I have the feeling that the rooms are getting quite narrow, and that my dress is brushing against everything. I have to go *sideways* through the door. In order to find peace, I wash everything off with Persil-water, and sometimes I also have to wash the dress that I happened to be wearing. Then everything becomes large and wide again, and I have room.

If I travel by train, I am constantly in fear lest someone in . . . might come aboard. If this happened, and the lady or gentleman were to come to sit somewhere near me, I would get off the train. Pictures in newspapers and magazines in which such things are represented disturb me too. If my hand happens to touch one, I must wash again. It is quite impossible for me to write down all the things that cause me alarm. I feel constantly in a state of inner agitation, and the nice adage: "Where you are not, that is where peace is" fits me exactly [p. 62].

This self-description is significant because it documents so vividly the shifting of the primary fear of death onto ever more external references to death. This is carried up to the point where the experience of the mortality of man is completely pushed back by the feeling of disgust; it is true that the latter, as Straus explains, regularly relates to decaying matter, but it is in no way limited to the dead and no longer has anything to do directly with one's personal death. Thus, a shifting of the actual complex of problems has come about, a transformation of the fear of death into a fear of that which is dead, decaying, falling into ruin. The central point is no longer contact and encounter with the dead as such; even letters and words have become quasi-contagious and thus threatening in and of themselves: they have, as Straus expresses it, "assumed the physiognomy of the decaying."

As an illustration, I offer the following example of an observation of my own:

Upon her entering my room, I asked a twenty-three-year-old patient who (because of a severe washing compulsion) did not like to sit down on a strange chair, where she wanted to sit. Her immediate reply was, "It does not make any difference, as long as no one in mourning has sat upon it. I detect everyone on the street who is in mourning; then I run across to the other side of the street. I would rather have myself run over by a car than touch a person in mourning. Even to pronounce the word 'black' is disagreeable to me, although, paradoxically, I like to wear black." This fear set in a year previously when she was invited home by the mother of a friend whose husband had died shortly before. She already had a washing compulsion at that time; her grandfather's death five years earlier had no effect of this sort on her; at that time, she even touched the dead man.

Another of my patients, who was likewise suffering from an obsessional neurosis, was "done in" for the whole day if he saw a funeral or a hearse. He felt on such occasions that it was so unesthetic for man to end in decay. He added: "It cannot be that everything is over at that time; that would be unfair. Some people are so callous that they step over corpses. Rationally, I know that everything is finished; Hitler and Stalin would then remain unpunished. That would be the meaninglessness of existence."

Here again the double aspect of death in obsessional neurotics is very evident. They are afraid of decaying matter and, at the same time, of death as a break, as "total death"—unexpected and final.

The fear of death and its variations, which are characteristic of the obsessional neurotic in the form of manifold fears of dead substances, or putrefiable matter, of dirt and dust, as well as his fear of the definitive, unrepeatable, and unforseeable nature of the course of life also manifest themselves in the relation of his ego to the external world. Checking on all occurrences with excessive alertness, the obsessional neurotic, like the phobic or hypochondriac, surrounds himself with safeguarding systems on a quite peripheral plane, as compared with his primary feeling of being threatened in his very existence. Safeguarding systems of that sort include counting and checking compulsions, obsessional orderliness and cleanliness— all of which make it impossible for him to abandon himself to the moment without fear of ordinary "perils." What results from this is an incapacity for enjoyment in the *hic et nunc* and, at the same time, a rigid attitude of ambition, which is directed to performance and/or an immaculate conducting of life. So strongly is the obsessional patient tied to this world that death by way of suicide does not even exist for him; every clinician knows this applies to even the most severely affected and tormented patients.

Anxiety Neuroses

Many fright reactions leave behind, for a shorter or longer period, a heightened readiness for anxiety. Such anxieties are mobilized above all before falling asleep, possibly as an equivalent of fear of the dark; they are, however, also released during the day under apparently ordinary circumstances. A patient wrote us, for instance, the following:

> Yet, at irregular intervals—chiefly in connection with headaches—the previous states of anxiety do return. Not in a form as severe as in the begin-

ning of June, but nevertheless strong enough to make me suddenly lose all my cheerfulness. What puzzles me in this is the fact that it occurs with words that signify death and illness, too, just as if I were allergic to that.

Recollections of life-threatening events that are cathected with anxiety may also be recapitulated by way of visual fantasies. A patient who had been treated for encephalitis for many weeks in the intensive care unit of the Neurological Hospital, and had received artificial respiration, continued for years to see with her "inner eye" details from the time she had spent there. The connection between this "compulsion to recapitulate" and the patient's attitude toward death became clear in the following symptoms: When she regained consciousness, she consistently addressed her daughter by the name of her beloved sister who had died early; later, she refused to wear, as she had done until then, the ring she had inherited from this sister.

During the course of neurotic reactions to horrible war experiences (Meyer, 1961a), it could be observed how, in ever increasing measure, unspecific stimuli were capable of evoking anxiety states of the same kind and intensity; the suggestion has therefore been made of using the term "fear-of-death neurosis" (Teicher) in place of "combat fatigue." If one traces the experiencing of anxiety back to its origin, one can almost invariably establish, as Schwidder (1959) remarks with regard to neuroses in general, that it is a question of residues of earlier experiences of fear whose representations in imagination were repressed. Schwidder raises the question of whether the individual experiences the basic limitations of the ability to cope as a narcissistic injury, so that fear is given the meaning of anxiety, which then has to be endured throughout life. Anxiety-neurotic symptoms in connection with nightmares and disturbances in falling asleep are very frequent phenomena among victims of National Socialism, who for years were forced to live in immediate danger. Their heightened anxiety-readiness brings about recurring, violent anxiety reactions to insignificant unexpected events, such as an unannounced evening visit or telephone call, traffic or driving incidents, or other situations even less unfamiliar (von Baeyer et al.; Eitinger). From this, the individual becomes housebound and frequently develops an avoidance attitude similar to agoraphobia. Anxiety dreams, too, belong here; generally, with the passing of time, they show a change and modification of the traumatizing event in the dream.

There are no doubt transitions and symptomatological similarities between anxiety neuroses and phobias. Basically, however, these are contrasting forms of pathological "anxiousness." In phobias, quite particular trigger situations evoke anxiety in an almost specific way, while other events that objectively are absolutely threatening are adequately mastered, and the person in no way appears fearful. One speaks, therefore, also of situational phobias. It is the other way around with anxiety neuroses, in which "just about everything" evokes anxiety; thus, a generally low tolerance for conceivable dangers characterizes the nature of these easily despairing, overanxious people. Schwidder (1959) therefore recommends, as a therapeutic goal, transforming diffuse anxiety back into concrete fears that the individual can face and then adequately react to. In phobias and hypochondriases, anxiety takes on a concrete form, whereas anxiety neurosis is characterized by a diffuse (irrational) anticipatory anxiety.

Depersonalization Neuroses

In a situation of deadly danger or following a very great fright, being injured or suddenly falling ill, or upon the death of others, experiences of estrangement (depersonalization, derealization)—that is, the sense of no longer being fully in touch with reality—may ensue. Such feelings of estrangement, setting in as acute reactions to a traumatic experience, range from emotional stupor of short duration[4] to lasting states of depersonalization, which shield the subject, as it were, from identical or similar anxieties.

A twenty-eight-year-old woman who had suffered a light cerebral concussion in a car accident was afterward still able to remember how the vehicle approaching in the opposite direction was crossing the green line on the freeway immediately before the collision. "I thought at that moment, 'I must not lose consciousness, otherwise I will not get off with my life.' Once I was back on the freeway, I regained consciousness. When I had my first

[4]The psychiatrist Baelz himself experienced, on the occasion of an earthquake in Japan, an emotional paralysis, calling it "emotional stupor."

visitor to the hospital—it was my father—it came to me that things are no longer the same. It is as if one were living in another world, as if one were already dead." During the course of an extended conversation, she added, "Sometimes I have a feeling as if someone, perhaps death, were waiting for me. I have been told that I am like my grandmother; my grandmother died quite young."

The patient's acute fright paralysis persisted for months; in seeking the genesis of this abnormal way of digesting a situation, one has to take into account her early childhood experiences in conjunction with the identification of death and the dead, which has an archaic tinge.

A fifty-year-old woman had been suffering from a depersonalization syndrome for as long as twenty years; it consisted principally in a change of the attitude toward her own body: "The entire person is a true misery. I feel insecure. It is a weaving up and down or a flickering in the whole body. When I move from the horizontal to the vertical position in the morning, everything appears dark and gloomy, even if it is a beautiful day. The whole body is disgusting to me." At first, the patient could not recall the beginning of this disturbance. Finally, she remembered how it began. She and her son had been spending half a year with her husband in a foreign town where he was working. She lived in a furnished room with kitchen privileges. The owner of the apartment, who suffered from abdominal cancer, was able to survey the kitchen from her bed; she would occasionally come unexpectedly into her tenant's room, frightening the boy. The patient felt enormously disgusted by the sickness of this woman.

In the first case, the depersonalization set in as a consequence of a vehement anxiety reaction to an accident that was witnessed up to the last moment and fully remembered, with the reality of the external world lastingly impaired thereby; in the second case, on the other hand, an encounter with a person suffering from cancer, which was felt as disgusting, brought about derealization, above all of the subject's own body. In both cases, the life histories show still other abnormal reactions (not discussed here) to situations that were experienced as embarrassing or threatening (see Meyer, 1959).

Another example of feelings of estrangement setting in acutely, which concern the patient herself, the people immediately around her, and the world at large along with them, stems from Heveroch.

A young signalman's wife falls into depersonalization when she learns that two lovers have had themselves run over by a train. The dead are constantly before her eyes; she cannot help thinking incessantly of death. The world no longer seems to be anything; it seems sunken and blacked out, unreal. She feels dead; her children, too, seem no longer truly alive.

We are reminded here that many victims, during the first weeks following their transportation to concentration camps, lived in a feeling of unreality, as if they were merely spectators at events that actually had nothing to do with them (Kral).

Among those depersonalization neuroses that make their appearance in acutely threatening situations is also the *phobic anxiety depersonalization syndrome* which, as the name indicates, consists of a combination of depersonalization and a phobic anxiety state. Roth found it to be induced in thirty-five per cent of his patients by the death or serious illness of close relatives, in twenty per cent by an illness of the individual himself.

Roth presents the example of a twenty-seven-year-old woman who one day was called to her father after he had suffered an attack of vertigo along with collapse. She reacted with apprehension, nervousness, and insomnia. Three weeks later, while waiting for her husband's return, she was informed by a policeman that he had been in a car accident. She heard the policeman's voice as if from a great distance and could only gradually comprehend that her husband had been but slightly injured. She no longer felt capable of any emotion. Her impression of being separated from herself and detached from the external world and of making every motion like an automaton—by an act of volition, rather than naturally and spontaneously—persisted for over a year.

Reactively induced experiences of estrangement such as this, which may persist for a long time, do not in every case presuppose a life-threatening or frightening event; they may also appear in the face of the need to arrive at a decision that the individual finds overtaxing. Particularly characteristic, however, is the connection with experiences of death and other catastrophes. In cases of this sort—and this should be stressed—a nonpersistent fright paralysis may be viewed as a useful, sometimes life-sustaining reaction in that it prevents the breakthrough of panic impulses to take flight and can thus make possible activity adequate to the situation. Only if the fright paralysis *persists* are we faced with depersonalization neuroses in the true sense.

In contrast to those forms of defense against fear of death that become manifest as phobias, hypochondriases, obsessional neuroses, and anxiety neuroses, the states of depersonalization signify a flight from reality into the seclusion of no longer being touched—that is, of isolation from affect. Thus, what occurs here, as a parallel to sleep, is a retreat from the consciousness of reality, which is simultaneously experienced as a kind of "being extinguished," and hence can be considered a symbolic anticipation of death. One pays for one's liberation from a deadly menace with an impairment of the feeling of being alive. The phrases in daily use: "almost dead with fear," "as if paralyzed by fright," characterize those complementary modes of reacting to overwhelming danger.

Addiction

This form of neurosis is being discussed last, for its obvious relevance to our topic does not at first glance seem clear. Certainly, oral gratification serves as a defense against anxieties of various types, but that the fear of death plays an important role here we do not learn from the patient.

From the psychoanalytic point of view, in drug

dependence it is a matter of oral wishes, which include sexual desire, need for security, and self-esteem. The world and its objects still retain the character of motherly nourishing; the addict behaves toward them like one who is a devourer (Matussek, 1959). He compensates for deprivations orally by incorporation, and this compensation occurs without delay. The fact that it *can* occur immediately endows this form of gratification with a somewhat euphoric character, even independently of the effect of the drug itself; it *must* occur immediately because of the fleeting nature of the effect and the danger of increasing deprivation. That is what constitutes the dependence. The important thing revealed by this is the addict's orientation *to the present*. He cannot wait; he has absolutely no threshhold of tolerance for mental stress; no time factor seems to exist, his tolerance being determined in each situation by his state at the particular moment. During the course of socialization, we learn to wait for rewards. This, in fact, is a mark of our fitness for social cooperation. The addict, as a result of the pleasure he achieves through the drug and the ease with which it can be reproduced over and over again, has lost that capacity (Rado, 1933, 1957). Whereas the obsessional, the hypochondriacal, and phobic defenses against the hostile, dangerous world—being wide awake to any possible threat—are concerned about the future, in addiction the individual's (artificial) defense against the world is a defense aimed at a present lack and not at all concerned with the future or the consequences for the future. " 'Nothing can happen to me.' Though his powers of reasoning and judgment appear to be otherwise unimpaired, he believes unshakably in his personal invulnerability and immortality" (Rado, 1933, p. 18). Of additional interest is that the addict, as Matussek (1952) has shown by the example of a gambler, calculates his chances on the basis of hazard,[5] whereas the obsessional neurotic dreads to an extraordinary degree precisely the chances that cannot be anticipated.

The absence of the time factor in defense—the urge for immediate gratification—entails a condition of importance to our reflections: the lack of circumspection—indeed, the lack of any consideration for possible dangers. The risk of traffic accidents, the risk of the addictive drug in regard to an adequate, sensible mastery of the tasks of life as they come up, and the risk to physical health—all these are taken for granted in a way that often appears fatalistic.[6] They are minimized or totally screened out. In the recent investigation by Stork on the circumstances of suicide among juveniles, frequency of accidents and dependency on drugs are characterized as equivalents of suicide. Many sayings and songs that are part of the atmosphere of the drinker reflect an attitude that is characteristically spoken of as "gallows-humor." From this one may infer that death as a future possibility does

[5] "Gambling with lucky chance is meant to make it possible for him to skip over his internal and external life-development and thereby to compress in this one instant the totality of historical time" (Mastussek, 1952, p. 250).

[6] Von Gebsattel (1948) speaks of the addict's "mania for self-destruction": "However, the possibility of self-destruction has merely a symbolic meaning to the destructive urge for self-annihilation operative in the depths; because self-annihilation cannot be carried out in fact, it is acted out in the pretense-realization of addiction" (p. 260; see also Zutt [1958]).

not "exist" for the addict, that no one else can deceive himself so thoroughly on the real dangers of life, and abandon himself so fully to the moment, as he can. This also becomes impressively evident in the passion for being thin, the *anorexia nervosa*, which in some of its aspects is correctly reckoned among the addictions. These patients, to our surprise, are not at all frightened when we talk to them about their life-endangering situation, even when we use such phrases as "we must not let you die."

This indifference of the addict to the future, his future life, and therefore also to death, is reflected, we think, in our general attitude to patients of this sort. In contrast to the suicidal individual hankering after death, who usually evokes a reaction of compassion, an angry rejection of the addict prevails; he is seen as frivolous, unreasonable, and weak-willed, and is held responsible for his fate and his misery. An additional viewpoint can be gathered from some self-descriptions by introspectively gifted addicts, a viewpoint that plays a not altogether insignificant role in the literature evoked by the drug problem of our time: alcohol, and above all drugs, may bring about a condition similar to the mortifying of the body (mortification) in asceticism (Huxley). In this sense, intoxication can be felt as an experience of the beyond, an anticipation of death, a relinquishing of the real world of life. Particularly impressive descriptions of such experiences occur in De Quincey's much quoted *Confessions of an English Opium-eater.*

Neuroses in the
Second Half of Life

Neurotic developments in the aging or elderly, although hitherto a rather neglected subject, are of particular importance to the question of the extent to which the problem of death enters into the psychodynamics of neurosis. A distinction must be made between the further development of a neurosis that had its onset before the middle of life and neuroses that manifest themselves for the first time in old age.

Longitudinal studies have shown that the *later course* of certain chronic neuroses shows a shift of symptoms or a mitigation of symptoms (Ciompi, 1969, 1972; Ciompi and Müller; Ernst). This is true of hysteria, anxiety neurosis, and neurotic depression; on the other hand, hypochondriasis apparently displays only very minor changes during the course of life. In obsessional neuroses, too, a mitigation of symptoms has been noted (Delkeskamp; Müller). With the exception of neurotic depression, similar findings have been made in clinical cross-sectional studies: beyond the fiftieth year of life, phobias, anxiety, hysteria, compulsion, or perversions are extremely rare; instead, psychosomatic and depressive neuroses completely dominate the field.

Neurotic depressions, depending on the specific life

situation, go through considerable oscillations; they are one of the characteristic psychogenic reactions of senescence and presenescence.

It is more difficult to deal with the *first manifestation* of neuroses at a later age. According to hospital statistics, there are fewer neurotics beyond the age of fifty (Ernst, et al.; Spiegelberg and Betz). A number of reasons can be given for this. One may lie in the difficulty in getting older or old patients admitted to a hospital unless organic cerebral disorders or deep depressive illnesses are present. If one looks at the occurrence of neurotic syndromes in general practice, there seems to be no question of a decrease of psychoreactive disorders during the second half of life. Shepherd and his collaborators have searched into the frequency of neuroses in general practice. The inception rates culminate between the twenty-fifth and forty-fifth years of life. The frequency plateau in the middle years is based on an accumulation of chronic cases *and* new ones; the latter distinctly decrease in old age, whereas chronic neurotics continue to be in medical treatment.

On the basis of systematic questioning of patients who visited a medical outpatient department, Pflanz found, interestingly enough, that older people, in contrast to their actual state of health, often complain very little. The age distribution of vegetative complaints, in particular, showed—with the exception of complaints about sleeping disturbances and constipation—a distinct decrease in old age. In the discussion of his findings, which certainly admit of more than one interpretation, Pflanz poses the question: Are there sociological causes that prevent an old person from taking "flight into illness?" One might also reflect upon the extent to which denial of being old, fear of death, and at the same time "consideration" for the physician seal the old person's lips.

The conditions under which psychogenic and psychosomatic syndromes of later life are formed are often easy enough for even the nonpsychiatrist to understand: they can be traced back to acute stresses. Among these syndromes are mourning reactions over the death of a spouse or of close friends, depressive reactions to the loss of one's job, to being pensioned off, to isolation from family life and social life, to decrease in income, and dependency on others. There are, further, hypochondriacal developments when a physical illness sets in or with declining potency (Kral and Gold). A small number of patients show the same neurotic syndromes they had in earlier years; what prevails now, however, is the picture of a flat depression with feelings of exhaustion, physical complaints worked out in part in a hypochondriacal manner, irritability, and sleep disturbances.

These simple depressive syndromes lack the marks of a genuine neurosis—namely, its defense mechanisms and the distance in time from the traumatizing event. Quite the opposite holds true of the former: in terms of motif as well as time, the reaction is usually confined to the specific life-situation of the old person. As to the question of a *first manifestation* of neuroses in the second half of life, it follows from the above that, whereas simple psychogenic reactions are frequent, neuroses in a narrower sense are almost totally absent.

How to explain that psychoreactive disturbances appearing for the first time in the second half of life present themselves in a comparatively monotonous form, and that as a rule there is no need for a detailed biographical exploration in order to uncover the more immediate genetic connections? The narrowing of personality dynamics, the slowing down of the rhythm of life (Petrilowitsch), and the waning of instinctual conflicts (E. Simmel) have been cited as reasons. Ciompi (1969) stressed the global quantitative decrease of instinctual energy, the "involution of libido." Thus, the neuroses of senescence seem to manifest themselves in exaggeration of character traits rather than in symptoms because instinctual conflicts fall away or at least progressively diminish in intensity. It could also be argued that sufficient stresses of all kinds are present within the first half of life—stresses that, in the case of a neurotic personality structure, bring about a manifest neurosis. Therefore, novel experiences and specific psychogenic reactions are no longer to be expected in later life.

Closer study of aging, of the course it takes, and of the circumstances surrounding it, shows, to the contrary, that aging and old age confront man in many respects with an entirely new situation (Pollock and Kastenbaum). Life in its external course is certainly familiar to him; what has changed, however, is his attitude toward his fellow men and the world around him. The further course of life can be foreseen; no longer, or hardly ever, can one count on unexpected favorable changes, on a revelation of hitherto undiscovered gifts or abilities, on new human ties. Life in terms of profession, family—often, too, in regard to one's place of living—is largely settled for the time that is left. It is difficult for the old person to attune himself to changes in the structure of the community and in his own social position, and to adapt to such changes.

At the same time, familiarity with death is growing; death has become a matter of waiting for it. One finds in old people, along with retrospection, an amazing number of anticipations of dying and death. When middle age has been reached, death becomes, as the psychoanalyst Jaques emphasizes, a *personal matter*. It is true, Jaques continues, that the unconscious per se is "unaware of death"; but there are unconscious experiences akin to those that in later life are consciously understood as pointing to death.[1]

We are indebted for the following observations to S. Gössling, who for years has been acting as director of homes for the aged. His observations illustrate the almost daily contact with death experienced among people of the same age and discussed by them without any shyness.

While the old person in the environment of his own home meets only with traces of death as he learns of the loss of a contemporary, hears about others dying and possibly attends a funeral, in the sphere of a nursing home another's departure from life takes place in a room nearby, or even in one's own room ... it is felt as a part of the

---

[1] "If the senescent phase of life has any element of value, its determinant can only lie in approaching death in the right way" (Guardini, 1953, p. 59).

"We find in old people. alongside their looking backward, a surprisingly large number of anticipations, including those of death. With growing years, thoughts about death become even more frequent in an amazing measure.... it is just as neurotic not to adjust oneself to death as a goal as it is in youth to repress those fantasies that are occupied with the future" (Jung, 1947, p. 218).

natural order and normal course of events and
constitutes the topic of daily conversations. In part,
this is surely due to the fact that the death of a
fellow inhabitant in a nursing home is connected
with quite concrete consequences for the others.
A place has become vacant—who is going to get
it? Someone who will be newly admitted? One
of the surviving inhabitants? "Place" in this context, stands for the bed, the room, the place at
the dinner table, and, no doubt, also the position the deceased occupied in his group. Often
enough, possible consequences of this sort are discussed with all their pros and cons even before the
final event has occurred. The old person in a home
for the aged sees and knows that he too must die.
Without having to be reminded, he is quite sure
that at some point it will be his turn. At least
after the lapse of a certain time, he comprehends
the immediate bearing the event has on his own
future. Any attempt to evade this knowledge by
way of the assertion, "Only the others—not I (as
yet), after all," founders on the unmistakable, occasionally even brutal, sobering remarks and hints
of the other group members.

On no account should one conclude from all
this that fear of dying is not known in homes for
the aged and nursing homes or that one can learn
there how to overcome it. But this fear has a different quality; it is more personal, more closely
defined, and, hence, probably easier to conquer.
An inner blunting may well have something to do
with this; but what is in the foreground is the
capacity for adjustment to facts that are clearly
part of one's own environment and existence.

It can happen that in addition to the repeated discussions within the group of the elderly in the home on death in general and the dying of individuals, is the need of an exchange of views with someone who is clearly not living under the same conditions. Discussions on the meaning of life with respect to its predictable outcome then predominate; on the connections between personal guilt, the course of life apparently ordained by fate, and dying as punishment for everyone; on the prolongation of life and the medical possibilities regarding this; on the chances for an easy death; as well as discussions of such reality-related problems as legacy and inheritance, or the shape that the lives of children and grandchildren are taking.

Only rarely does it occur that one or several fellow-occupants of the same room expresses the wish that someone who is dying be transferred to a single room, or an isolation room, in order to be moved away from them.

On the contrary, I have often heard the opposite wish—that is, the express request not to make any transfer, to leave the dying fellow-occupant in the room until his death. I do not think that curiosity about a process customarily hidden from view underlies this, or the endeavor to render final service. Rather, these people feel that enforcing a separation would be unnatural and something they would not like to be exposed to one day.

It will have to be left undecided to what extent the way of dealing with dying and death described here is generally true of old people, or regularly to be met with in old-age homes. It is particularly noteworthy that here, "at the last station" too, the fear of *seul mourir* weighs heavily. Besides, there are, as we have seen, mainly two conditions that bring about a progressing concretization of mortality, two conditions that intensify each other: one's own fragility and need of help, on the one hand, and on the other, witnessing over and over again the deaths of those of one's own age. Both these experiences are probably common to all human beings; the way they are worked through, however, depends on factors that lie much further back than aging and old age. It seems, for instance, that it is particularly difficult for those who have matured late to accept the fact of being old.

We therefore take issue with the hypothesis that the second half of life must confront man, as a rule, with the same, or at least quite similar, problems as the first half of life. What we observe in the psychiatric sphere indicates the opposite: modes of adaptation that were adequate in earlier phases of life are adhered to, even though they are no longer appropriate. This is especially true of self-protective mechanisms, which are continued even though they do not prove helpful in dealing with the new perils, above all in the confrontation with death. This rigidity brings about what we call exaggeration of character traits in old age—the transformation of thriftiness into stinginess, for example, or of caution into suspicion, of independence into stubbornness. Dealing with death is made even more difficult by this consolidation of attitudes and conduct that stem from youth and early adulthood. Ohlmeier and Radebold, in their endeavors to develop an analytic group therapy for elderly and old people, became especially aware of regression as a defense mechanism.

In drawing a conclusion about the problem of old-age neuroses, we may start out from the following facts: The neuroses that have appeared in the first half of life tend toward symptom mitigation in old age. The number of neuroses appearing for the first time in old age is small, and limited almost exclusively to simple hypochondriacal and depressive reactions, as a rule in immediate undisguised connection with the specific psychic and somatic stresses of that phase of life. In spite of the fact that old age imposes new tasks and privations for which the first half of life has hardly, if at all, prepared us, no neuroses appear in old age that would be worked out and find expression in the structure and symptomatology corresponding to the neuroses of early life.

What could be responsible for this fact is the transformation of the inevitable sense of the finiteness of human life into a genuine, realistic fear of dying and death. The psychogenic symptoms of hypochondriacal character as well as the reactions to loneliness point almost directly to the old person's current anguish. "Evasion and taking refuge in anxiety about one's body—an anxiety that is placed, as it were, in front of the fear of death—are at the bottom of many a hypochondriacal-depressive disorder" (Schulte, 1962, p. 96). It is also significant that the ambivalence of death wishes and feelings of guilt usually characteristic of mourning are generally not found among the mourning reactions of old people (K. Stern et al.).

On this basis we form the hypothesis that the growing awareness of approaching death no longer admits of repression or evasion, thus preventing any formation of specific old-age neuroses; it "permits" only simple psychogenic reactions, and contributes to the symptom mitigation of neuroses that had already become manifest at an earlier phase.

To be sure, the certainty of dying, which at best can still be actively denied, does not constitute the sole explanation of the phenomenon, puzzling as such, of the absence of specific old-age neuroses. Our hypothesis does appear, however, to be well-founded for still another reason.

Every neurosis contains in its genesis the element of "future"—future as uncertainty and task at the same time, as symbol of our one-way passage through life, whose irreversibility frightens us, as sum total of those so far unforeseen possibilities to which we might abandon ourselves. The neurotic symptom protects us from the necessity of dealing with the future or, correspondingly, of having to change. In this sense, old age has no future, no *uncertain* future.

Psychodynamic Aspects— Provisional Conclusions and Discussion

On the basis of the preceding presentation of various forms of neurosis in terms of their relation to fear of death, the following conclusions may be drawn:

1. Experiences with death are not infrequently encountered as precipitating or causative factors *before* the onset of a neurosis.

2. Some forms of neurosis show, *at the point when* they become manifest, a massive fear of death which changes to circumscribed worries and fears as the neurosis develops, therewith losing the character of a reaction to a vital threat. Fear of death is calmed down, coded, repressed.

3. In neuroses of greater severity, the attitude to mortality also seems to be included in the neurotic process (in the form of repression, distortion, and exaggeration).

Ad 1: Our observations of adults in terms of confrontations with dying and death *before* the manifestation of a neurosis, even in the individual case, admit of only limited statements about the pathogenic relevance of such experiences. Their effects may be unspecific, in which case they have no determining influence on the type of the psychogenic illness. In the case of an obsessional neurosis, for instance, we will have to ask ourselves whether the illness would not have made its appearance in the same way and at the same moment if the future patient had—to mention two very different examples—accidentally stepped into feces on the street, or if he had suddenly been forced to make a disturbing, yet inescapable decision. It cannot be overlooked, however, that in dealing with certain neuroses—especially the phobias, hypochondriases, and obsessional neuroses—one learns with striking frequency of such experiences with death. Do they become more lasting, selectively remembered, as it were, because of the specific structure of the neurosis, or have they exerted a decisive influence on the manifestation of the neurosis and thereby come to possess an immediate genetic relationship with it?

Ad 2: Through the examples given, it has presumably become clear how, from a fear of deadly peril, which initially completely dominates the individual, there develop, in the course of time, particular fears, pseudorealistic anxiety. Avoiding certain situations overcathected by anxiety characterizes the phobias; excessive body relationship with its concern about the functioning of organs is typical of the hypochondriases; and indefatigable watchfulness in defense against possible dangers of the present and future is characteristic of the obsessional neuroses.

In the anxiety neuroses, the defense is effected in an inverse way: earlier "frightful" experiences fall into oblivion and their place is taken by anticipatory anxiety, which is fearful of "everything." The fact that here the flight from anxiety is not taken into the details of specific situations as it is in the phobias, or with painstaking defensive measures, as it is in anancastic personalities, probably has to do with the predominantly hysterical structure of the anxiety-neurotic; among the elements of a hysterical character belongs the retreat from reality—"leaving the field" in the face of any concrete danger.

Depersonalization syndromes, which likewise generally appear in persons of hysterical character, usually set in suddenly as fright reactions. Here, the avoiding of danger takes place in so drastic a manner that the patient has the impression of vegetating as he would in a dream, as if he were lifeless. This sort of disturbance may be of a cognitive nature (alienation of the perceptual world: derealization) or it may manifest itself as ego-disturbance (depersonalization).

In addiction, the dominating factor is obvious indifference to the mortality of man. The addict shows himself to be indifferent to the further course of life and its risks and is given to minimizing whatever lies in the future. Fear of death as such does not appear, but the toxic elation may be experienced as a deathlike state—as a "small death."

Ad 3: Basically there are two inadequate attitudes to death, to the "absent presence" of death: one lies in overrating death—death that is possible at any time—and leads to all the manifestations of anxiety, such as avoidance, caution, vigilance, and "checking" on everything. The other lies in overrating the "now," in trusting that death does not exist, somewhat along the lines of the saying, "So long as we are, death is not." Straus (1930) points to the polar contrast between addicts and phobic patients, with regard to the attitudes toward death and being threatened: The gambler, "while still daring to challenge fate, no longer confronts it as a doer and shaper of things; rather, he simply accepts its decision, be it happiness or annihilation. At the end of this line, there stands the phobic, who breaks down in anxiety if he so much as catches a glimpse of the Existential by way of the spatial characteristics of width, depth, narrowness" (pp. 74-75). If uncertainty and the unimaginable nature of personal death are prevalent, this is linked with an attitude that has to do exclusively with a lack of concern for the "now" and its real dangers, with an urge for immediate gratification. Such is the mark of addiction. One goes on living as if even the morrow were in doubt, as if it were fruitless to worry.

Anxiety, caution, vigilance are strategies of avoidance vis-à-vis death and the many different ways in which it can approach us. They cause the disparity between anxiety and real threats to grow ever larger. In the case of the obsessional neurotic, it is possible for the obvious relation to deadly danger, to the magic aspect of the association with the dead, to the nonreversibility of our course of life[1]—it is possible for all these relations to remain in existence without going through a process of repression. In some obsessional neurotics, a fear of death is so domineering a theme that the old term *thanatophobia* appears justified. In these cases, fear of death is not the basic root of anxiety, which is comprehensible as a reaction to our mortality; it is rather its neurotically sharpened form and its isolated exaggeration. This exaggeration con-

---

[1]Fenichel (1945) comments, "'Orientation in time' is a typical reassuring measure. Many a fear of death means a fear of a state in which the usual conceptions of time are invalid" (p. 285).

sists, as becomes clear in Skoog's case described earlier, in the omnipresence of death, so that the patient feels continuously surrounded and almost devoured by it. If the term phobia, which is now generally used for the situational phobias, also seems appropriate for thanatophobia, this is because of the condition of the mortal human being, upon which the patient ponders incessantly—a situation that has here, so to speak, lost its distance in time.

The example of thanatophobia shows us that the problems surrounding death do not appear in the neuroses solely in the form of diffuse anxieties or of circumscribed fears, but that fear of death as such— once the character of uncertainty of personal death disappears—can also shape the clinical picture of a neurosis.

In addiction, on the other hand, it is precisely the regard for the future details of one's life and for all the questions about death—its when, how, and thereafter—that are missing. Instead, not only is the future disregarded, but at the same time an anticipation of death occurs in intoxication, in torpidity, as is to be seen in many variants, from passing euphoria to suicide or to self-destructive addiction. One may thus speak of "too little" fear of death, of a denial of the problems of mortality, at the same time as, in a quasi-frivolous manner, death is anticipated. The conditions are similar in the alienation syndromes in which fear of death is certainly warded off by means of the abatement of vivid feelings, yet a deathlike state accompanies this process.

However, we have to call attention to the fact that some writers have regarded as useful, even absolutely necessary, a *partial* repression of death. Max Scheler, for instance, spoke of the vital usefulness of the repression of death and warned only of an "over-normal" repression, which then results in fear of life. Zilboorg (1943) emphasized the necessity of death-repression with regard to our social functioning: under normal conditions, in non-neurotic persons, fear of death appears only in a mitigated form and modified; "If this fear were as constantly conscious, we should be unable to function normally. It must be properly repressed to keep us living with any modicum of comfort."

Our own observations of adult neurotics let us down to a great extent, so far as the evaluation of experiences with death in *childhood* is concerned. We know from adopted children that the real or alleged death of their biological parents (as a reason for the adoption) is often imperfectly assimilated and may lead to massive neurotic symptoms (Peller). Besides, an encounter with dying and death may occur, in the mastery of which the adults leave the child to his own resources or try to calm him by using euphemistic metaphors; under these conditions, the encounter will continue to persist as an unmastered trauma. Under the influence of comparable experiences, neurotic symptoms then develop in adolescence or adulthood. For instance, there may have been in childhood nothing but a temporary, albeit obstinate, fear of the dark, and as late as at the beginning of adulthood a washing compulsion sets in.

According to Muensterberger, even the infant's fear of the separation from the maternal breast signifies fear of "the final separation from life," and Winnicott points out that anxiety, as early as in the first stages of parent-child relationship, has to do with fear of annihilation. A view that is to a certain degree parallel to these ideas is to be found in Bowlby's *"primary anxiety,"* which he considers to lie at the bottom of separation anxiety. At first, this is fear of abandonment; during the course of child development it is complemented by (acquired) fear of experience. Where the family is disturbed, fear of death appears even in small children—under certain conditions as early as in the third year of life. Only a child who is protected by identification with strong parents is immune to fear of death. From this, Wahl deduces that the fear of death is of basic importance in the origin of neuroses, and he regards neurotic symptoms as symbolic substitutive attempts at binding the anxiety. There are in the literature many instructive examples of thanatophobia in later childhood, in which memories of funerals are often recapitulated. The *parallelism of death and sexuality*, in regard to the process of becoming conscious, as well as to curiosity and repression, has been pointed out, by Hall (1915), for example: "The psychology of death has very much in common with that of love, especially from the new genetic and psychoanalytic viewpoint .... As the first naive infantile curiosity about sex is soon powerfully repressed, so the first interest in death suffers multifarious *Verdrängungen.*" (See also Fenichel.) Adults tend to avoid both themes as a whole. This goes hand in hand with the use of language intended to make them seem harmless.

Why is it that the problem discussed here—that is, the question of the significance of our attitudes to death with regard to the genesis of the neuroses—has

hitherto hardly been discussed by psychoanalysis?
Freud's conception of the death instinct, because it is
rooted in speculative thinking, has been met almost
solely by criticism, even on the part of his followers
(Bromberg and Schilder).[2] Freud's statement that no
negation exists in the unconscious (1915), on the other
hand, has found general acceptance and has led to the
belief that wherever we find fear of death, it is
concealing other unconscious thoughts; it is the equivalent of worries that all people have in common, of
pain or guilt, of being deserted, or of loneliness. The
basic approach of psychoanalysis sees the "cause of all
ills," from birth on, in the beginnings of life, in the
early experiences of separation fear, and later on, of
castration fear. The fact that death quite early plays a
role in the child's life has obviously gone largely unnoticed, as has the fact that death—as will be discussed later on—between the eighth year and puberty
becomes step by step subject to a process of repression
that in many respects runs parallel to the development
of sexual taboos. Finally, there is the added factor that
psychoanalytic therapy was—and is—used almost exclusively with persons in their first half of life, and
that, consequently, very little experience has been
gained about neuroses in old people.

Up to the present, death has been given little attention in *psychiatric* literature—far less, in any case,
than has suicide. This is surprising, not only in view of
the growing importance of gerontology and geriatrics,
but also in view of the fact that during the last decade

[2]See also, Brun; Caruso, 1952; Flügel; Money-Kyrle.

phobias and anxiety syndromes have been studied with special intensity.[3]

With the exception of Melanie Klein's work, one finds in psychoanalytic literature only a few papers that, in their observations, interpretations, and conclusions—for the most part cautiously formulated—come close to the view advocated here. The importance of the fear of death and its repressions stands out most clearly—in the writings of Money-Kyrle, Muensterberger, Wahl, as well as in those of Loeser and Bry,[4] who have especially studied and treated phobic neuroses. Riviere (1932), too, has stressed the importance of this. She says: "We cannot escape the conclusion that an intense fear of dying by active aggression or passive neglect is a fundamental element in our emotional life, is as deeply-rooted in our unconscious minds as life itself and is barricaded off from conscious experience by every known mechanism of defence" (p. 166). In this connection, we must also mention Matussek (1948), who deals with the attitude toward death from a different viewpoint. He remarks that Freud (1900) regarded as relevant to the genesis of obsessional neuroses only the death of close relatives which, out of the ambivalence of love and hate, is often experienced as being one's fault. Matussek (1948) emphasizes that, when an individual who is totally

[3] Williams has investigated how often death, suicide, and homicide have been the subjects of studies. Marks's monograph of 1969 leaves the fear of death altogether unmentioned.

[4] "To claim that death fears are not a factor in the unconscious is to ignore a vast body of knowledge derived from anthropology, sociology, and studies of religion" (Loeser and Bry, 1960).

committed to the empirical world is confronted with
death as the limit he cannot "transcend," he may
develop neurotic symptoms. Neurotic despair arises
precisely from experiencing the idea of one's own
death as consisting of the annihilation of existence and
mind. Modern man, no longer a believer, is always in
danger of being wrecked—that is, of fleeing into
neurosis—whenever he is confronted with death unprepared, for he is unable to assign to dying a meaningful place in his scheme of the world. As Matussek
puts it, "Rather, one recognizes that in the fact of our
natural end, there lie the most varied opportunities for
the genesis of neurotic symptoms" (p. 126).

Psychoanalytic literature has thus heretofore offered only a narrow basis as a point of departure for our
hypothesis. This may be because the problem of death
lures one so easily into metaphysical speculations, and
psychoanalytic tradition quite rightly shuns the danger
of straying away from its empirical basis into such
trains of thought. Stern (1972) says, "It is surprising
that psychoanalytic psychology, despite its characteristic tendency to uncover the hidden truth behind all
denials and repressions, nevertheless, in its studies up
to this day has rather neglected the fear of death, our
steady companion." The author considers working
through the fear of death to be an indispensable part
of every treatment, for he sees in the failure of adaptation to this fear an important cause of neurosis. The
fear of dying is interpreted as fear of the return "of the
(physiologic-) biotraumatic situations that every small
child has suffered" (p. 901).

The reflections presented here, however, can
hardly be charged with being metaphysical specula-

tion. They explain the experiences of clinical psychopathology and are wholly guided by the principles of psychoanalytic thinking. Indeed, they could not have been undertaken at all without that orientation.

Psychoanalysis has always not only dealt with the analysis of instinct dynamics, but has also gone beyond this. It is faced with the necessity of including anthropological considerations, which, along with the dynamics of instinct, overlaying and influencing them, are of significance to the development of life. With regard to the problem of death, Freud (1915a) stated: "Would it not be better to give death the place in reality and in our thoughts which is its due, and to give a little more prominence to the unconscious attitude towards death which we have hitherto so carefully suppressed?" (p. 299).[5]

Accordingly, we have to try to complement those aspects of death which are the result of current general attitudes with a description of the mental climate; for, since this is the background for specific psychodynamic problems, it is not without bearing on the problems of death with which the individual patient is involved.

---

[5] Freud's opinion about the relationship of the fear of death to early anxieties may also be of interest in this connection. In "The Ego and the Id" we find the following: "[The ego] sees itself deserted by all protecting forces and lets itself die. Here, moreover, is once again the same situation as that which underlay the first great anxiety state of birth and the infantile anxiety of longing—the anxiety due to the separation from the protecting mother. . . . The great significance which the sense of guilt has in the neuroses makes it conceivable that common neurotic anxiety is reinforced in severe cases by the generating of anxiety between the ego and the super-ego (fear of castration, of conscience, of death)" (1923, pp. 58-59).

Current Conscious Attitudes
Toward Death and Dying

Social and personal attitudes make comprehensible why our thoughts about death are concentrated more on the uncertainty about when death will occur and on dying alone, or on whether there is life after death. In so-called "primitive" societies, where life after death is a certainty, man's thoughts may turn to passing the test in dying, to a heroic end or an end met with composure. In the Middle Ages, man's doings on earth were judged by the standard of whether they complied with the Christian commandments, thus affording to a certain extent a guarantee that he would, at the Last Judgment, escape damnation and the wrath of God. If the modern western capitalist society is characterized by the high valuation accorded to achievement and the striving for success, this signifies, with regard to the problem of death, that great, indeed decisive importance must be ascribed to the uncertainty about the length of time we will live, and that the time left to us may therefore become the "measure of all things."

"I do not think about dying because I do not have the feeling that I am very close to it."

"Why, indeed, should I think about it? Only sen-

timental people do so. I have my life to live, and it
does not leave me any time at all to concern myself
with that subject."

"In my opinion, we have to put up with death,
there is no sense in wanting to run away from it. Not
that I concern myself much with dying, but I do know
that some day it will be my turn. I just try to give my
life as much content as possible and to make use of my
time. I think this is the only course one can take."

"I do not want to talk about it. I do not at all see
why I should. Is there any reason to? All of that is still
so far away; at least I hope so. It is true, one never
knows quite exactly, but I have that certain feeling. I
mean, I know that I still have time. After all, I am still
young. You do understand me, don't you?"

These four replies to an interviewer's question
about the attitude toward death, taken from Dichter's
book *Strategy in the Realm of Wishes* (1961, pp.
176-180) (written from the point of view of marketing
psychology), demonstrate quite accurately the stance
that characterizes the current personal (and public)
attitude toward dying and death. The fact that all
men are mortal is driven out of our everyday life; it is
pushed aside, eliminated from consciousness. Everyone, it would seem, cooperates—to use Freud's words
—"in killing death by silence," in taking death for
granted, and thoughtlessly acquiescing in it. At the
same time, these answers reveal the anxiety that is
deep down under the surface and which imbues the
minimizing attitude to the subject. Characteristic in
this respect are, above all, the "self-reassuring" questions directed to the interviewer. The four quotations
reflect various degrees of complete—or, as the case
may be, incomplete—repression.

In the public life of our modern world, there are numerous indications of the correctness of this so-called *hypothesis of repression*.[1] It is striking, however, that this hypothesis is often championed by its adherents with an enthusiasm that has all the earmarks of a confession of faith, of a conservative cultural criticism, rather than its being the outcome of a careful consideration of all relevant factors. Even though in recent times the theme "dying and death" is evidently gaining in interest, this can hardly cause any basic changes in the notion that our life as it is at present, set against the background of technical-scientific progress on the one hand and the loosening of binding religious convictions on the other, leaves no room for an intensive grappling with death. "The 20th century is simply too busy to be much concerned with the problem of death and the beyond," according to an English publication of 1908 (Choron, 1967); or, critically expressed: "The social ignoring of death in developed industrial societies represents less a symbol of freedom than a sign of a widespread lack of freedom resulting from nonthinking" (von Ferber, 1963, p. 343).

Mourning

If we proceed from the consideration that the death rites of the early history of mankind served mainly as a protection against the dead, whereas they now serve to

---

[1] "Dying is shoved away, not as if one wanted so much to live, nor, however, as if one somehow wanted to look into what is coming, or to let it be seen. . . . One lives thus for the moment; no thought is to be given at any point to the worst that is yet to come" (Bloch, 1959, p. 1299).

comfort the survivors, it is evident that we are being less and less permitted to mourn. In this context, mourning is to be conceived of as the opportunity for giving the loss we have suffered symbolic, visible, socially acceptable expression.[2] Although the important subject of "the inability to mourn," is the title of a book[3] that, by virtue of its political and moral deliberations has become widely known, there is nowhere in that book any discussion of death and of mourning the dead by the survivors. Not even the question about the relation between mourning and death is raised.

Gorer's study of *Death, Grief and Mourning in Contemporary Britain* (1965) has made clear what a burden it places on the survivors to be forced—as a rule, quite alone—to decide in what way to mourn. Without rules of conduct for the survivors and those around them, a situation of isolation around the mourners arises today, as if it were actually obscene to show grief. Gorer demonstrates how good friends openly avoid a mourner, or are offended if the latter refuses an invitation because of his frame of mind.

In modern industrial society, the mourner has no status (Bally, 1967; Fuchs). The gradual disappearance of funeral ceremonies, established as they were in every detail, leaves the individual concerned particularly helpless if he is unable to give personal expression to his grief. Gorer considers it therefore absolutely

[2] The more than four hundred *Kindertotenlieder* (children's death-songs) written by Rückert, after two of his children had unexpectedly died, are a particularly well-known example of mourning in literature.

[3] Mitscherlich, A. and Mitscherlich-Nielsen, M., 1967.

indispensable to develop secular forms of mourning that will assure the mourner both "privacy and companionship." "Modern man is expected to maintain the aggregate of his social functions undisturbed by the occasional accident of losing a beloved person, just as he is expected to depart from life without causing a disturbance" (Eissler, 1955, p. 42). Modern man no longer has much opportunity to "become accustomed" to death. The changes in funeral rites, which originally accomplished some of the work of mourning, have been a chief contributing factor in removing dying and death from the field of vision of the living and in making it impossible for man to have a lifelong familiarity with dying.

In mourning we not only give expression to the loss we have suffered. With it, we are able—and probably precisely in its ritualized form—to live through and add to the experience of death (Fulton). The prayer at the graveside for the one whom death strikes next, makes this quite clear; it includes the opportunity for some anticipation of one's own death. If, in our time, we seem to be ever more prevented from mourning, this change in our forms and opportunities for giving visible expression to our grief appears to constitute further proof of the hypothesis of repression. "What happens to all emotions—the proscription of whatever does not have any market value—happens most drastically to that from which it is impossible to draw even psychologically a restitution of the ability to work, that is, to mourning. It becomes the stigma of civilization, becomes asocial sentimentality, which gives away the fact that committing mankind totally to the empire of purposes has not yet been entirely successful.

... In truth, on the dead is inflicted what to the ancient Jews was the most horrible curse: 'not remembered shalt thou be.' It is on the dead that men vent their despair over no longer remembering themselves" (Horkheimer and Adorno, 1969, p. 255).

It seems easy to establish a connection between the changes and liberalizations of dying ceremonies and funeral rites, on the one hand, and "de-Christianization," on the other. Sociological studies on the funeral director in the United States have made it evident that there, as generally in highly industrialized western countries, the effort to render death harmless for the sake of better functioning has advanced farthest. At the same time, however, it is in the United States that "funeral reform movements" came into being and found considerable resonance in public opinion; it is there, too, that the most careful and comprehensive researches have been carried out on the death problem of the present time. The two anthologies *Death and Identity* (Fulton) and *The Meaning of Death* (Feifel) as well as the sociological study *Awareness of Dying* (Glaser and Strauss), constitute convincing evidence of this. They are without parallel in other countries.

With regard to our question about the significance of death for the origin of neuroses, it would be of the greatest interest to learn whether and to what extent the banishment of dying and death from the life of the community—that is, the making a private affair of death—has caused changes in the neuroses of our time. Concerning such a historical transformation of the gestalt of psychic disorders, however, hardly any reliable data are at our disposal, especially as far as psychogenic and sociogenic illnesses are concerned. One may, it is true, speculate that the changed attitude toward the finiteness of human life must affect the type and frequency of neuroses. But if we consider the manifold and radical cultural and social changes that have taken place *at the same time*, we cannot be surprised at our not yet being able even to estimate approximately the significance of the death problem with respect to the frequency and modes of manifestation of the neuroses.

Religious and
Philosophical Considerations

Within the context of our investigation, we also
have to ask in what way twentieth-century theology,
philosophy, and psychoanalysis have defined their
attitudes to death and the mortality of man. The
transformation that has taken place within a few
decades from a "death-philosophy" to a diminution of
the importance of personal death at the hands of dialectical materialism may appear to social critics to be
an unmistakable indication of modern man's lack of
any standpoint. Regarding the question of how it is
possible for the individual in modern society to adopt
an attitude to death, the discrepancy between theoretical concepts and convictions is indeed highly significant. This is true even though the statements of the
theologians and philosophers are not readily accessible
to the understanding of the general public; they seem
to exert, in distorted and coarsened forms, at least
as strong an influence as does the development of
modern medicine and natural science, which is easier
to grasp.

Christianity and Theology

The attitude of Christianity to dying and death results historically from three diverse and in part contrasting traditions: the severe inner-worldliness of the Jewish Yahweh faith, the Greek idealism of the immortal soul, and the belief in resurrection as found in the New Testament. In the Old Testament, birth and death are strict boundaries enclosing life. Death is an evil ordained by divine judgment, but it is also the definitive ending of a life fulfilled. The inexorable fight against any cult of the dead in ancient Israel is a consistent expression of this attitude. The doctrine of the immortality of the soul, with which the Greek world from Homer to Hellenism is imbued, continued to exert its influence by way of the Christian church and finally came into prominence again in a modified form in the Age of Enlightenment and in German Idealism.

Up to the beginning of this century—including, therefore, the time of the reformers—a more formal distinction was made between resurrection and immortality; but in their essence the two were conceived of as largely identical and were contrasted with the "this-worldliness" of the Jewish faith. It is only in our time that it has been emphasized in theological quarters that a *complementary* relationship exists between the realism about death of the Old Testament and the belief in resurrection of the New Testament. In practical ministerial care and in part also in dogmatics, elements of the idea of the immortality of the soul are even now still prevalent. Trillhaas comments in this connection that it is a strange view of modern theology that the idea of immortality is a threat to the purity of the belief in resurrection. He characterizes the idea of immortality as a primeval phenomenon. For instance, speeches at the grave, in order to give comfort to the survivors, are generally only about the soul of the deceased having "gone home," expressing the sentiment that we may confidently leave this soul to the love of God, that the deceased is not alone, but closer to God than we are.

Under the influence of existential philosophy, death became, in Protestant but especially in Catholic theology, termination and fulfillment at the same time. "In death, existence places itself at the boundary of all being, suddenly awake, knowing and liberated" (Boros, 1964). Death, then, is not nothingness, but rather the eternal substrate from which we have come. In this spirit, Tillich (1959) says, "There is no time after time, but there is eternity above time" (p. 33). Or von Balthasar (1956): "Eternal life is no second life different from the earthly and finite one, but it is its eternal width and depth, eternal in God" (p. 299).

The dualism of body and soul has long been prevalent in Christianity and in the ideas of the Beyond of most religions; now the doctrine of *total* death is set against it—a doctrine of which the belief in resurrection is an inseparable part. Resurrection is an act of the grace of God, in the transfiguration of the body comprising the whole human being; through this act man is led to a new and other existence. Christ's resurrection has opened up the possibility for all men to partake of eternal life (Barth). At the same time, modern Protestant and Catholic theology, referring to the Gospel according to St. John, are formulating ideas of an anticipation of the "hereafter," of

judgment, purification, and resurrection, as the pre-
senting eschatology.

The ideal of a "natural" death, characteristic of
Marxism, now also appears occasionally in Protestant
theology, as, for instance, in the formula: one has to
react to the fear of death with care for life; it is true
that it is for God to limit the time of life, but man has
the right to die a natural death. "To spend one's entire
life as a practice for dying is a scandal. It was due to
pagan influence when in Christianity too an *ars
moriendi*, 'an art of dying,' was developed.... Natural death has to be worked for—politically, socially,
medically" (Jüngel, 1971, p. 161).

In the Christianity of the present, death has lost the
cruel character it had, especially during the fourteenth
and fifteenth centuries;[1] at the same time, however,
there has been a paling of the image of a Beyond
resembling the fields of the blessed in contrast to the
earthly vale of woes. What is most important in all this
for man today is the fact that with the doctrine of total
death the contradictoriness of the death experience,
the thought of the impossibility of anticipating one's
own death, has become even more pronounced; for so
long as man was certain of the immortality of his soul,
he did not need to be oppressed by his inability to
imagine his no longer being on earth.

From the psychodynamic viewpoint, one also has
to ask oneself what the consequences may be of the
modern polarization of resurrection and the belief in

[1] The severity of the preachings in those times can be inferred
from the example of God's judgment in *The Husbandsman from
Bohemia* by Johannes von Tepl (1967): "Every man is in duty
bound to give his life to death, his body to the earth, his soul to
US" (p. 80).

immortality. As we explained earlier, the horror of "total death" lies precisely in the extinction of psychic existence. Is not this radical ending of our life going to direct man's attention even more intensely to the continuance of existence immanent in the world and, with this, to lay claim on him even more fully?

Existential Philosophy

It is not possible to discuss the spiritual situation of present-day society in relation to death without taking existentialism into consideration; for in all the history of philosophy, there is hardly another movement that has dealt as intensively with the problem of death.

Death here becomes the central point of reference for human life; as early as with Kierkegaard, this is quite evident. He calls man's despair the "sickness unto death," and says that never to have felt despair is the greatest misfortune; to be seized with despair is a true gift of God, even though it is the most dangerous sickness if one refuses to be healed of it. The double meaning of the *concept of "Verzweiflung"* (despair) as used here by Kierkegaard is more closely differentiated in Tillich's exposition (1969) on *"Zweifel und Verzweiflung"* (Doubt and Despair) in the light of the threat to our spiritual life by way of "emptiness" and "meaninglessness." "Were it not that man disappears, I as Being would be endless permanence and would not exist. . . . I lose existence if I take Being-there as an absolute, as if it were Being in itself. . . . Death is for every existence the necessity of its Being-there" (Jaspers, 1965, p. 220).

In despair turned unto death (despair as indispen-

sable human experience), we have touched upon the
core of existential philosophy. Life or Existence (in this
philosophy) is always only Being in relation to death.
The existential concept of death is on principle incom-
patible with any form of the idea of the Beyond, just as
much as it is with Freud's doctrine of the death
instinct, or with the "nullification" of personal death
by ideologies that leave the individual continuing to
live, but only in his people, his class, or his society.
There develops in existential philosophy—sometimes
with a pretentious pathos, which Adorno (1964) has
criticized as the "jargon of authenticity"[2]—an *ars vi-
vendi sub specie mortis* that comprehends death as an
entirely personal death, in each case "mine." In this
context, Luther is quoted: "Alone we are summoned
to death, and none will die for another." In this sense,
the death of others does not signify a useful experience of dying; it can, according to Heidegger, at best
represent a substitute theme for the finiteness of man's
existence. Death as an everyday occurrence can even
lure us into evading Being by flight into death. Nor is
"being sure about death" to be equated with believing
death to be true, as the final possibility of our existence. Knowing about death, "this ingredient of his
nature—that of being human," does not liberate any
man from his pure finiteness (Tillich, 1969). Existential philosophy is, however, less concerned with concrete death than it is with "Being toward the end,"

    [2] "What is conceivable is a social state in which men no longer
have to repress death, in which they could perhaps experience it
otherwise than in anxiety—this mark of a crude, primitive
condition that Heidegger's doctrine has immortalized in supra-
naturalistic words."

which shows itself in the existence of man as a *being* creature (Heidegger).

Jaspers emphasizes man's *ambivalent* attitude to death. Seeing death as friend and foe, simultaneously longing for it and avoiding it, he writes, does not represent a conflict of man with himself. In Sartre, the meaning of death is given an additional, more radical, accent: he does not regard death as his own, as personal in each case, but rather sees it as the "turning into nothing," the annihilation of all possibilities, depriving the individual—as if through condemnation—of any significance.

In existentialism, the importance of the *hora incerta* comes clearly to the fore; Sartre, for instance, realizes that we are unable to wait for death (*attendre la mort*), but can only prepare ourselves for it (*s'attendre à la mort*). It is only with advancing age that waiting for death becomes possible, for the uncertainty of the hour of death lessens at that time. Basically, however, the "when" of the indefinitely certain death can be at any moment.[3] We also encounter the misery of dying alone, when Jaspers

[3]"We know about the 'That', but not about the 'When' or the 'What'; it is crucial, in this, that the 'When' may be at any moment and that the 'What' by the nature of things can not be learned. Thus death stands for man in a twilight of both knowing and not-knowing" (Plessner, 1951, p. 377). G. Simmel (1918) says: "This. . . . shows how absolutely determining death is to the shape of life, how death infuses life with what is certain about it, as well as with what is uncertain. In the fact that this boundary is plainly firm and yet at the same time plainly fluid in our consciousness, in the fact that any manifestation in the one as well as in the other would immediately change our entire life in an inconceivable way, death reveals itself as that element that is seemingly on the outside of life, while in truth it is within it" (p. 106).

stresses the loneliness of death for the dying as well as
for the one who remains behind. According to Sartre,
in death I "fall prey to the survivors." Death is not
obliteration of consciousness or annihilation of the
world; rather, in relation to the others, it is my "fall
out of the world." In Sartre's discussion of Heidegger,
he stresses that Heidegger's "in every instance personal
death" has led to every detail in life being given this
character of the personal—that is, of something of
which no one can relieve you; in fact, much can be
done by others for you. Death is not "possible for me,"
it is rather an annihilation, a "bringing to nothingness
of all my possibilities," (1952, p. 676). "Since death
does not appear on the substrate of our freedom,
it must deprive life of any significance" (p. 679). In
Sartre (as well as in Tillich) birth and death are
equated with one another: "Death, like birth, is a
pure fact; it comes from without and transforms
us into without. Basically, death differs in no way
from birth, and the identity of birth and death is
what we term *Geworfenheit*, ['the character of being
thrown into this world or out of it']" (Sartre, 1952,
p. 687).

It is important for our theme to be quite clear
about the theories of anxiety of the existential philosophers, theories that are closely connected with their
conception of death. Kierkegaard tells us that anxiety,
as a manifestation of the possibility of freedom, is at
the same time an expression of the wholeness of human
nature. In his distinction between anxiety and fear,
Heidegger demonstrated that our everyday attitude
toward impending death is often no more than a flight

from the thought of death and clearly betrays our striving for "undisturbed indifference." Thinking of death and the assured conviction of one's own mortality are not sufficient. They are inauthentic forms of the fear of death and the flight from death; anxiety is contrasted with them. Anxiety alone as a basic state of mind of *Dasein* (being here) is for Heidegger an expression of the belief in death; or, in other words: in anxiety, the mortality of man reveals itself. Death as a limiting situation, in Jaspers' case, calls forth two forms of anxiety: anxiety of *Dasein* (being here) about an inauthentic, miscarried life, and existential anxiety of the radical Nonbeing.

Existential philosophy in the form of existential analysis has gained an entry to psychiatry and temporarily came to occupy a commanding position in psychiatric-theoretical thought, although its approach could hardly be put into practice in therapy. In existential-analytic psychiatry, Minkowski, Straus (1930), and above all, von Gebsattel (1954) took up the philosophically central death-aspect, and made use of it in the interpretation of psychopathological phenomena and life-historical developments.

Dialectical Materialism

The direction of existential philosophy, which sees the existence of the individual in terms of man's mortality, appears to dialectical materialism to be characteristic of the entire misery, the theological passions of bour-

geois society and its philosophers of doom.[4] Such an
evaluation of death (including, for example, Socrates'
willingness to die) is, dialectical materialism declares,
expressive of a society that does not fight death with all
its might in order to prolong life. Thus, a brute
biological fact is transformed into an existential privi-
lege. Indeed, death has been turned into an element of
submission, of resignation in face of those who are in
control. With this, in Marxism, death becomes the
mark of bondage and defeat. In view of the immortality of mankind, from now on the goal of all efforts
must be to attain "natural," "elemental" death. That
means ridding humanity of death by violence, just as
was demanded in the Age of Enlightenment. Philosophy ought to react to the fact of death, says Marcuse
(1968), with a "great refusal."[5] This would allow man,
after a life fulfilled, to die at a time of his own
choosing.[6] "The gradually increasing duration of life
may change the substance and character not only of
life but also of death. The latter would lose its ontological and moral sanctions; men would experience

[4] "Theology and philosophy are today competing in glorifying
death as an existential category; in turning a biological fact into
an ontological essence, they bestow their ontological blessing upon
the guilt of mankind, which they help to gloss over" (Marcuse,
1968, p. 220).

[5] An inscription on a wall in Paris of May 1968 read: "La mort
est nécessairement une contre-revolution" (quoted according to
Marti, 1969).

[6] "In a life no longer distorted and denying, a life that would
no longer defraud men of what is theirs, they would probably no
longer have to hope in vain that life would after all grant them
what had been withheld from them.... But, from the fact that
men repress death, it cannot be inferred that death is the essence"
(Adorno, 1964, p. 128).

death primarily as a technical limit of human freedom" (Marcuse, 1959, p. 69).

According to Bloch (1959), in view of the inescapability of death, life acquires its special meaning
through man's works, which outlast him. This is also
valid in the case of the person who, because of his
class-consciousness, because he has overcome his indi-
vidualism, is able to die without anxiety. An elemental
death, as Bloch remarks at the close of his chapter on
"Pictures of Hope against Death," could even be
replete with contents pointing to the future—contents
that would make death no longer the denier of the
utopia, but rather the denier of anything that is not
part of the utopia. "In the content of death there is no
longer merely death, but the uncovering of life-con-
tent that has been gained" (p. 1389). For Adorno, too,
a state of society is conceivable in which men would no
longer be compelled to repress death, but would be
able to experience it without anxiety.

In Bloch, we find at the same time, however, the
almost prophetically formulated conviction that death
cannot be overcome by social liberation, but rather
that in a liberated society—one without poverty and
anxiety—"the concern about death arises with particular poignancy." "The accommodation with the subject of society," he says, "has succeeded in classless
society, but the hypothetical subject of nature from
which death comes lies in another area, wider than
that of the social harmony that has been achieved"
(1959, p. 1381). The degree to which Bloch is confronted with this problem and tries to tackle it can be
seen by his formulation of 1968: "Whence, then, the
courage in face of immediate death, this ending that is

at one and the same time most democratically general, and yet a most misanthropically leveling process?" (p. 336).

The thinkers of dialectical materialism, in discussing a natural, anxiety-free dying, often take a step further in envisaging the possibility of one day totally overcoming death in a repression-free society. "The inescapability of death does not disprove the possibility of an eventual liberation" (Marcuse, 1968, p. 2); and "Therefore, in view of the potential of control over organic processes, a potential of which the outline is becoming visible, the idea of the abolition of death cannot *a fortiori* be disposed of. It may be very improbable; yet, that is conceivable which, from the existential-ontological point of view, could not even be admitted to thought" (Adorno, 1964, p. 130). Fuchs (1969) places his wide-ranging study expressly under the aspect of "natural" death as standard and aim. He closes his exposition on the advances of medicine and the "old-age guarantee" made possible by them with the following words: "These amateurish comments on the avant-garde of the mastery over nature had the sole purpose of illustrating what potentialities society possesses even now for making itself in ever growing measure the master of death" (p. 179). I shall later discuss how far, precisely because of the latest medical developments, the possibilities of perceiving and materializing a "natural" death have come increasingly to present a problem for medicine.

In the attitude to death, dialectical materialism reaches a position which, strangely enough, appears similar to that of those who, without critical reflection on the resulting consequences, celebrate medical and scientific advances and predict a development having no limits. Guardini in 1961 expressed this common attitude in the following formulation: "In recent years acceptance of death has largely taken on a form that can be characterized as nothing other than capitulation. Man has to a great extent given up his protest against death because he can no longer bear the constitutive conflict, as it might be called...; this has taken place in closest connection with the biologization and socialization of existence, which is gaining ground everywhere" (p. 398). No less critical are Gollwitzer's pronouncements: "When man in a changed society no longer sees his riches in material wealth and power but in his fellow-men, it is a complete illusion to think that, having recognized this as his true happiness, he will find his own dying and that of others more easily bearable" (1971, p. 51).

Psychoanalysis

The most important contribution psychoanalysis has made to the problem of death is Freud's hypothesis of the *death instinct*. In "Beyond the Pleasure Principle" (1920), Freud took as his point of departure the tenet that an instinct is "an urge inherent in organic life to restore an earlier state of things" (p. 40). It would be in contradiction to this "conservative" and "retrograde" nature of the instincts if "the goal of life were a state of things which had never yet been attained" (p. 41). On the contrary, a return to an old state, the state from which the living entity has departed—that is, a return to an inorganic, inanimate nature that was in existence before the living organism—must be attained. It is in this sense of the return to an inorganic state that "the aim of life is death." The sexual instincts aim at propagation and the continuation of life; the ego instincts, in the last analysis, at death. Freud's view, which he himself expressly termed a "speculation," culminates in a clear dualism of ego instincts as equal to death instincts, and sexual instincts as equal to life instincts. From the start they wrestle with each other, even though at first the life-preserving libidinal forces are largely dominant over the destructive death instincts (later on also called "instincts of aggression").[7]

In addition to Melanie Klein who, on the basis of her reflections on the death instinct, postulated the existence of a fear of annihilation in the unconscious (1948), it was actually Federn (1932) who made an effort to incorporate the hypothesis of the death instinct into the theory of the neuroses. In his study on the reality of the death instinct he says: If we know ever-threatening death, anxiety actually becomes a signal of imminent physical death—"a signal that causes the operation of the death-instinct to be felt as a [immediate] threat of death, and not only to be [continuously] feared" (p. 364). In accordance with Freud's second theory of anxiety (1926), anxiety is dealt with here as meaning both a breakdown of the pleasure principle and a biological warning signal; this characterization is applied to the fear of death, of which it is simply stated that we know it. This "knowing" is taken to be a conscious process: the fear

[7]This polarity has been formulated by Mitscherlich (1961): inasmuch as hope is what the libido outlines for the future, it is a true opposite of what *destrudo* predicts—that is, death.

of death is to be understood as fear of dying—that is, as fear of the physical death that is threatening. In general, the attitude of psychoanalysis may be characterized as being: death is accepted as a biological process that renders possible the cycle of organic life. "If we are to die ourselves, and first to lose in death those who are dearest to us, it is easier to submit to a remorseless law of nature . . . than to a chance which might perhaps have been escaped. It may be, however, that this belief in the internal necessity of dying is only another of those illusions we have created 'to bear the burden of existence' " (Freud, 1920, p. 45). Death appears to be without significance for the individuation of man, as has been stressed by Jung. It is, on the contrary, only in a biological sense that death is the aim of life. There is no kinship to the conception of human life as a "Being under the aspect of death"; there is, in psychoanalysis, no allusion to any conceivable overcoming of death as an ultimate potentiality of future development. Nor does the striving for a natural, anxiety-free dying appear in a direct form. Psychoanalysis, then, has on the whole attributed minor significance to death.[8]

Some of Sartre's ideas and some thoughts in recent theology seem to open up an opportunity for overcoming the apparently unresolvable contrast between the viewpoints of psychoanalysis and existentialism, and thereby for transforming these alternatives into a new, complementary concept. Tillich (1959) comments that

[8] Bowlby's important psychoanalytic work on separation anxiety, in its section entitled "Grief and Mourning in Infancy and Childhood," deals only with the mother's breast, which in weaning is withdrawn from the child, and with the separation from the mother; it does not deal with death.

it is just as hard to imagine Not-yet-being as No-longer-being. On this, Job, 1, 21: "Naked came I out of my mother's womb, And Naked shall I return thither." Between these two boundaries, life takes its one-way, irreversible course. Does it not follow from this that all man's early experiences can be understood as being terminal experiences at the same time?

Results of Empirical
Social Research

In this section, we shall report in some detail on the great number of studies that, in recent decades, have concerned themselves with attitudes to death. In contrast to the theoretical concepts arising out of theology and philosophy, these investigations, guided by pragmatic viewpoints, offer insight into present-day attitudes to dying and death. This does not admit of separating the factors determining those attitudes into distinctly personal and social ones. What otherwise must rightly be regarded as a shortcoming in terms of method, proves to be an advantage in that it presents a supplement to the cultural-historical background by means of the information supplied on the individual in his environment.

In these social-empirical studies, the attitude to death is dealt with in terms of its dependence on social factors as well as on other variables. Some of these variables are: age, self-esteem, religiousness, human ties, physical and mental health. In addition to questionnaires and semistandardized interviews, projective-test procedures were mainly employed; new word-association tests were often developed especially for this purpose. We have arranged our survey according to age, and it is only in conclusion that we shall discuss objections that can be raised in regard to method and the uncertainty of the interpretation of results.

Childhood

The studies on the age-dependent change in the child's attitude to death show a large measure of agreement. Between the ages of one and three, death means to "depart" (*disparaître*) and is conceived of as an existence maintained under different conditions. Between the ages of five and nine, the notion of personal death appears in the child's mind. Between ages nine and ten, or perhaps even a little later, death comes to be understood as a biological factor, an irreversible dissolution of the body; with this, the child joins adults in their modes of thinking and habits of expressing themselves. This sequence, essentially defined by Nagy, is found as well in Gesell, and in Anthony; above all, in regard to the time at which man's mortality and, with this, one's own death enter the child's consciousness (see also, Alexander and Adlerstein, 1958). The eighth year is the true turning point in the process of assimilation of the notion of death—a process that is concluded by age twelve. At that point, if development is undisturbed, with the acceptance of man's mortality, the childhood ideas of magical omnipotence disappear, as do the feelings of responsibility and guilt in relation to the death of others. It is only in late childhood that the naively realistic assessment of death and curiosity concerning the circumstances accompanying dying, which are strikingly similar to the child's attitude to sexuality, give way to the adult's conventional notions. Although Fuchs is certainly right in warning of the speculative supposition that the child, in the process of socialization, repeats the history of mankind, still, there are two remarkable parallels between children and primitive societies (Lévy-Bruhl):

1. Children (between the ages of five and nine) do not always distinguish clearly between death and the dead; among primitive peoples, too, fear of death is very often not fear of death but fear of the dead—fear of their return and vengeance.

2. Children (of about the same age) see death not, as we might expect, as a natural process—that is, as the effect of illness or growing old—but rather as the effect of violence and hostility. This violent character of death is, by the way, quite often also encountered in the fantasies of adult neurotics. Primitive peoples do not seem to know of natural causes for falling ill and for death. Violent death and its equivalents—in the shape of being transformed by magic spells, being poisoned, and being devoured—are met with as a *leitmotif* in fairy tales everywhere (Snow White, The Three Little Men in the Woods, Little Red Riding Hood, The Seven Ravens, Sleeping Beauty).

Adolescence and Early Adulthood

Among college students, almost without exception little death anxiety was encountered. There was no clear difference between those who had religious ties and those who held nonreligious convictions, although it is true that the latter reacted faster with death anxiety to stimuli, even when these were not specific; about fifteen per cent of the college students probed could be characterized as "death-concerned."

In investigations of this sort, when a word-associ-ation test was combined with the psychogalvanic skin reflex, distinct differences appeared in children from five to nine years of age as compared with youths between the ages of thirteen and sixteen: in contrast to what happened with the children, the results of the skin-resistance measurements among the youth were more striking than was the extension of the reaction time in relation to "death words." On the whole, death is experienced with increasing affect from kinder-garten age up to student age—with the exception of the latency period (see also the studies of Alexander; Alexander and Adlerstein, 1959; Kastenbaum, 1959; Middleton). "It seems strange that, at that period of life when both vitality and viability are greatest and the will to live seems to have its maximal momentum, the death-thought is so prone to be obsessive" (Hall, 1922, p. 445).

There is no research dealing *exclusively* with youth (puberty and adolescence) and its attitude to dying and death. It would be interesting—among other things, in view of the high incidence of suicide during the period between puberty and complete maturity— to investigate from this viewpoint the process of psy-chic maturation after puberty has set in; for in no other segment of life do we encounter so intense an urge for full self-development in the present, side by side with such intense orientation toward the future.

At no other time of life are the present and the future dominant at one and the same time, while the past seems removed from the field of vision.

The Middle Years

The results of research into this period of life are least uniform. The usual questioning is capable of ascertaining merely superficial conventional attitudes. It was not even possible to establish positive differences between the attitudes to death on the part of normal persons and of psychiatric patients.

Bromberg and Schilder interpreted the results of their investigations of people between the ages of twenty and fifty-two, to the effect that the thought of death, in contrast to the ever present positive attitudes to life, reaches an individual only by intricate paths. Dying is experienced as dismemberment and castration; death appears as a way out of unbearable life-situations, as an appeal for the sympathetic attention of others, as ultimate narcissistic fulfillment, and as self-punishment. The mode of questioning on the part of these writers, as well as the age of those who were selected for study, suggests the thought that it was mainly suicide that was meant by death, in these instances.

Growing Old and Old Age

The most important mechanism of adaptation to growing old in those over fifty seem to lie in conscious denial of death; a more realistic attitude to death is encountered about equally often. With advancing age, the number of those who accept finiteness increases, as does the willingness to talk about death with one another. Lieberman and Coplan were able by way of psychological-test evidence to ascertain differences in this respect. These differences were dependent on whether the old people died within one year, or only after three or more years: more fear and concern with dying appeared when the life expectation was shorter (more death symbols in the TAT). The death attitude of older people also showed differences that were dependent on religiousness and social integration: those who were living with their families or in old-age homes showed a more positive attitude to death than those who were living alone (Jeffers et al.; Munnichs; Rhudick and Dibner; Swenson, 1961, 1965). Evidently when man is living under favorable conditions, out of gratitude for his earlier life, he is more capable of accepting future suffering, whereas with scanty social contacts and a difficult life situation a greater readiness for illusionary hopes is found to be present.

Of the various patterns of adjustment to old age described, the following seem to be true: Active individuals for whom the stress always has been on performance achieve the greatest contentment in old age if they can retain part of their previous activity and are able to carry it through; in the case of the more passive and family-related, on the other hand, "disengagement" becomes the optimal life style.

Reichard and his collaborators,[1] who divided more or less successful adjustment to old age into five modes,

---

[1] Here one finds a very vivid example of a mature adjustment to old age: "I try to work like I was going to live forever, and I try to live like this was my last day."

found calm acceptance, anxious recognition, or a "counterphobic activity," each in one-third of the cases. Corey distinguished four ways of dealing with the awareness of mortality: avoidance, acceptance, neutralization, suppression. Among this group of old persons, the posture of avoidance was particularly frequent, whereas in young people acceptance and neutralization were found equally often.

In summary, we may state the following: We have at our disposal quite subtle knowledge of the development of the child's attitude to death. The taking-over of the modes of thinking and expression of adults that begins in later childhood comes to an end in puberty, while at the same time the death theme as an existential problem reaches its highest degree of importance. Studies of attitude, moreover, make it evident that in old age, especially in the last years of life, man is increasingly conscious of death. The extent to which this consciousness, particularly in conversation with young people, is expressed as conscious denial or as a more realistic attitude of acceptance depends on the individual as much as on the attitude of the people around him. It is possible, on the other hand, in cross-sectional studies as well, to define types of old people with respect to their attitude toward old age and dying; these types, too, are to be linked up with personality and earlier life history, but at the same time with the current social situation. It is in the case of adults that the study of attitude yields the least uniform results; they give information, as has often been stressed, about the public opinions of those around them rather than about their own fundamental fear of death (Jeffers et al.; Lester).

In a recent study, Handal and Rychlack have

found a higher percentage of anxiety and death dreams to occur not only in groups with greater "death consciousness," but also in groups with a "death consciousness" that was below the norm. This result in the case of those with a slight "death consciousness" might support the repression hypothesis. The method applied in attitude research does not for the time being admit of expressing a firm opinion on whether these repressions are to be attributed to tabooing of the topic by society or within certain age and social groups, or whether it is rather a manifestation of a *personal* defense when responses to stimulus words suggestive of dying and death are delayed or do not emerge at all.

With regard to our hypothesis of the pathogenic role of the attitude to death in the genesis of the neurosis, it follows from the investigations cited above that it is only in late childhood that adult notions of death are adopted. In consequence thereof, the child is up to this point particularly vulnerable to neurosis-inducing influences on the part of persons with whom he has a close relationship—influences that are rooted in their attitudes to dying and death. If in the adults closest to the child a neurotically repressed death anxiety prevails, which expresses itself, for instance, in anxious, phobic overvaluation of everyday dangers, the child lacks internalized norms for dealing with death, such as may be needed when someone close to him is dying.

Modern Medicine and the Elderly and Dying

During the twentieth century, developments have taken place in medicine that have altered our relation to dying and death. The technique of artificial respiration has made it possible to maintain mechanically functioning circulation and breathing in unconscious patients; consequently, from the points of view of medicine, of law, and of theology, the serious question arises of whether the individual concerned is still actually alive or has already died—a question that often cannot be answered unequivocally for days on end. Organ transplants are carried out successfully with increasing frequency and are gradually becoming a routine method capable of keeping alive over a long period of time patients who have hitherto been incurable.

Apart from these extraordinary possibilities, created by highly specialized clinical medicine, there exists, because of the growing life expectancy, a similar situation in general medical practice as well: in Germany, for instance, between 1900 and 1970, and allowing for the decimation caused by the wars, life expectancy rose from thirty-four to seventy years! In the future there will be an ever growing number of old people whose intermittent sicknesses will have become easier to control. Both processes, the "artificial" prolongation of life by means of organ transplant and resuscitation, as well as the "natural" prolongation of life by way of an elevated life expectancy, have in extraordinary measure intensified the question about a "natural" death at the end of a fulfilled life. What is involved here is the difficulty, often apparently unsolvable, of deciding what the right conduct is, on the part of a medical profession that feels committed to humanity. "Right conduct," in the case of unconscious patients as well as of gravely ill old people, takes in the question of whether and to what extent it is justified or defensible not to apply this or that possible medical measure for the prolongation of life when there is not even a limited chance for recovery.

Decades ago, pathologists were already finding it difficult to form a judgment on the aging of organs, to diagnose a natural biological death brought on by old age. At that time a concept of illness based purely on biology prevailed in medicine. The psychosomatic concept of illness, extended as it is through the inclusion of psychogenic illnesses, has complicated the problem and rendered it more difficult. But the question about a fulfilled life transcends even the horizon of psychosomatics. What are the criteria by which, today and in future times, the physician is to judge when life has indeed been fulfilled and whether or not the patient wishes to die? "It is our paradoxical attitude toward death, not the fact of death itself, that makes insoluble conflicts seem inevitable" (Weisman and Hackett, 1965, p. 327).

What seems to be the case is this: it is only under unbearable pain or—quite exceptionally—in a situation experienced as fulfillment that the old person is capable of recognizing that the moment of his choice has come. What would the decision be if the patient and his physician had to regulate their conduct according to the postulate of "natural death"? If one is serious about the view that it is essential to die an anxiety-free, natural death at the moment of one's own choice, this can actually only lead to the result that dying as a personal task is experienced as an even heavier load; for, to the gravely ill person who is incurable, the worry about the burden that his care and need for help could mean for his relatives is thereby increased.

Among the points that have to be considered in connection with modern medicine and the present socioeconomic conditions, belongs, in addition, that birth and dying have to an ever greater extent been transferred from the private sphere of the home to the institution of the hospital. This means that dealing with the dying patient has been in large part delegated to a cast of professionals. More than half the population of the United States no longer die at home or in an old-age home, but in a hospital.

Psychiatric, psychological, and hospital-sociological investigations in the United States have been able to show how the relations of physicians and nurses to a patient change as soon as it has been established that he is going to die (Eissler; Glaser and Strauss). It is a change that must be characterized as a formalization and neutralization of the relations, as an avoidance of direct human contact, masked by technical measures and instructions. In the case of patients in a radiation department—in old-age homes, to some extent, as well—the topic of dying is strictly tabooed, even though all the patients are aware of their fate and talk about it among themselves (rarely, however, to others). Not infrequently, a relationship prevails between staff and patient that Glaser and Strauss have described as a "ritual drama of mutual pretense." How far modern man has drawn away from a conscious dying becomes quite clear if one compares it with the traditional Catholic death chamber, with its prayers, extreme unction, the cross of death, and the rosary in the patient's hand—prepared quite openly and as much "in time" as possible.

In this connection the important question follows of whether and to what extent the incurable or dying patient has a right to learn the *truth*.[2] Is it that the physician conceals from the patient his imminent death because he himself would experience this as an infringement on his own feeling of omnipotence and as a narcissistic injury? As for the relatives, the "fateful course" cannot be hidden from them in any case, so it is better not to withhold any information from them. A myth exists, partly induced by the patient, of the physician as conqueror of death. It may therefore be a question not so much of whether the patient can tolerate the truth, but of whether the physician can bear to tell it to his patient.

In an essay entitled "Denial as a Social Act," Weisman and Hackett express the view that most physicians reinforce their patients' tendencies to repress. Often the dying person himself fleetingly gives

[2] On truth at the sick-bed: Aldrich; Chodoff, Kübler-Ross; Moore et al.; van Oyen.

up his death repression, and that only *vis-à-vis* some-one who is not important to him. Nonetheless, the physician ought not consider it his duty to break down "at all costs" his patient's posture of repression; repression often seems to be the only way adolescents and young adults are able to bear dying.

In Germany, as well as in most other countries, it is a rule not to inform the person concerned—or at best very vaguely, although one does make the situation clear to his relatives. But recent investigations have made it impressively plain that contact between the dying person and his relatives is rendered difficult when there is no suspicion on the part of the former and full knowledge on the part of the latter of what is impending. The relatives who feel obliged to exercise self-control and self-denial withdraw from the patient, leaving it to the medical profession to deal with him. It is obvious that the *extreme* discrepancy customary with us between the unknowing patient and his informed relatives is precisely what is responsible for the fact that the patient's isolation sets in quite some time before his death. In the hospital, it is then usually a night nurse or some "night sitter"—completely strange to the patient—who, instead of his relatives, attends his dying, after he has been separated—generally without a word—from his fellow patients. For avoidable as well as unavoidable reasons, "taking leave," which could give the dying person and his relatives one more opportunity for direct contact has become quite rare.

The English-speaking investigators mentioned above come to the conclusion that it is advisable for the physician to explain the incurable patient's situation to him in such a manner that the patient can assess his condition correctly, if he is capable of accepting this. On the other hand, the patient who is not in a position to learn the truth, or even remotely to suspect it, will interpret the very same information as confirmation of the chance for recovery. That seems indeed a good way to proceed, for if the patient understands the "message" it leads to an alliance with the physician that is capable of sustaining stress and may preserve the relation to the patient's relatives by relieving both parties of the burden of "sparing and concealing," of false consolation. On the basis of experiences and reflections of this sort, we may conclude that one should refrain from unilateral disclosure of terminality to the relatives; the more so since in many cases the physician cannot honestly give any exact information about the moment at which death will occur. It is precisely this real uncertainty about the "when" that enables us to avoid the great discrepancy between the information received by the patient and that received by his relatives, and thereby to avoid his too early isolation.

In German literature, this idea is intimated by Plügge who speaks of the "Pythian answer" that the physician should give to the incurable patient. Beyond our daily hopes with their disappointments, says Plügge, another hope becomes possible, one that transcends our existence.

There is a further viewpoint that should perhaps be taken into consideration when we are dealing with incurable patients and with the dying. In the hospital, there is strong pressure on the patient to exercise self-control. A rejecting attitude is the reaction shown and displeasure is more or less openly expressed when patients in their suffering behave "regressively"—that is to say, when they moan and complain. Chodoff has stressed how important it is to the gravely ill patient to be allowed regression to dependence and non-self-reliance. Cancer patients in particular fear, as he was able to observe, that one might gain the impression that they are not "pulling themselves together." If Norton, an American psychoanalyst, was apparently able to help her patient, who seemed particularly afraid of being left alone to die, she could do so because—among other things—she did not prevent the patient from yielding to this regression (no doubt promoted by the patient's becoming blind). Our hospitals, with their impressive technical equipment, would be more humane if they more willingly accepted suffering and dying in the form of open despair or of a need for help expressing itself in childlike ways.

The vivid report by Kübler-Ross, and especially the careful studies by Glaser and Strauss on patients who are dying in a hospital, contain most instructive descriptions of the roles and interactions of nursing personnel and the unsuspecting or suspicious patient, the denying patient, or the knowing one who openly accepts his imminent death. It would be highly desirable for physicians and nursing staff to know about these processes, the meaning of which is not always readily grasped; the patients and those to whom they have entrusted themselves for treatment and care would benefit thereby.

All that has been said here should have made it clear that dying today is, to an especially high degree, dying alone. By admission to the hospital and within the hospital, in consequence of the staff's attitude

toward death as well as of the information given
unilaterally to the relatives by the physician, the dying
patient is also externally isolated. In this connection,
we have to mention the fact that the attempt made by
Kübler-Ross to find new ways of communicating with
dying patients was violently opposed by the medical
profession. The following results of a study by Kastenbaum (1965) are perhaps also to be interpreted in the
sense of a repression of death on the part of physicians:
Kastenbaum asked for an estimation of the probable
time of death in the case of one hundred old patients;
throughout, the life expectancy was overestimated,
although the physicians questioned were familiar with
the diagnosis in each case, as well as with the typical
course of illness in this geriatric ward.

The longevity of men who today die early less often
than they did in the past entails their often being able,
and being forced at the same time, to anticipate death.
It is the "dying alone" and the necessity of adjusting
oneself to it in the midst of an environment that is
largely denying death that characterizes the present
situation.

Society and the Individual and Their Approach to Dying and Death

Repression—a term frequently used in this treatise—
takes place on different levels, and quite diverse
circumstances are given this label nowadays. To begin
with, "repression" is a technical term of psychoanalysis
meaning the (normal or neurotic) excluding of an idea
or feeling from consciousness, a process that takes

place unconsciously. Suppression, on the other hand, is a goal-directed process of avoidance that takes place consciously and is usually supported by reasons. In society there are more or less obligatory "public" attitudes that are related to repressions, as well as suppressions, in a way we as yet hardly understand. Further, theoretical concepts exist that are the result of thought processes in individual persons, and often reach the consciousness of society only after having gone through manifold selective processes and simplifications. These concepts determine the "spirit of the age," or they alter it, and then, in their turn, bring about the repression of trains of thought that do not harmonize with them.

These processes certainly appear to apply to the problem of death. Dying, death, mourning have increasingly become a personal, private matter which should be of as little concern to society as possible. Von Ferber (1970) speaks of "making a private matter" of all notions of the Beyond: "The peculiar disproportion between the anthropological significance of death and its representation in our culture ... can hardly be disposed of as a self-created problem of cultural criticism" (p. 245). The hospital has to a great extent lost its charitable function. The dying person still experiences "comfort" there, even if his condition can no longer be changed decisively by the possibilities of modern medicine. The institution "Hospital," the large number of persons who (dividing their labor) attend to him, and the gulf between the relatives and the "unsuspecting" patient—all this leads to an early isolation, before the *seul mourir*. The reducing and deritualizing of funeral customs and mourning habits, the euphemistic ways in which death is spoken of in death notices, at the grave, in front of children, are obviously designed to veil man's finiteness, the fact that death can take place at any moment, and to lessen the impact of that fact. The topic of "death" is thus treated in the thoughtless noncommittal manner in which one speaks of things with which one has to reckon "anyway." It has frequently been stressed in recent times that it is only as a biological event or as an object of statistics[3] that death is still openly discussed nowadays; for one may argue, in the case of younger persons and those of middle age, death generally represents an event today that, owing to technical-medical advances, one can succeed in avoiding.

Modern medicine seems almost in a position to guarantee a course of life that will reach senescence undisturbed (Fuchs). In view of this, it is understandable why the higher life expectancy together with the growing proportion of old people in the population have not been instrumental in stimulating a coming to grips with the problem of death; for the most important precondition for "natural" death, the guarantee of old age, has been fulfilled. In a theological publication dated 1971, we can read the following: "One dies today, as a rule, old and satisfied after a long life.... I have, in recent years, buried almost exclusively old people. Death appears today in most instances at a time when the arc of life quite naturally curves back to earth. Grief and mourning stay within stipulated boundaries" (Bauer, 1971, p. 56). Evidently, one for-

---

[3] "Death is misunderstood by an era that has become addicted to facts, because death, being the transcendent fact which breaks through the world of empirical reality, is understood as an empirical fact" (Metzger, 1955, p. 193).

gets completely that the latest advances in medicine do not, of course, come to a halt with the treatment of old people; rather, there arise, at that point, problems about prolonging life or alleviating dying—problems for which there are as yet no reliable standards in modern medicine. The attitudes toward death even in old people are, as we have seen, determined in a considerable measure by their fear of dying and of dying alone. Hence it follows—we think, inevitably— that reaching the age of dying represents only one part of the way toward the goal of dying a "natural" death—a part that does not render it any easier for us to reach a decision about the kind and extent of our therapeutic efforts. It is even to be suspected that "natural" death is a *new euphemistic term*, which in the last analysis eventually conforms to those modern tendencies that (in accordance with the repression hypothesis) avoid a confrontation with the problem of death. If attaining "natural" death is proclaimed to be an important sociopolitical goal, even a first step toward a no longer inconceivable "overcoming of death" (!), what is expressed thereby is basically nothing other than the endeavor to push death off into old age and to minimize it for those in old age.

It seems further worth noting that there are hardly any empirical clues to indicate whether or how far our attitudes to death depend, among other things, on the question about the "hereafter"—whether it be in the form of resurrection or of immortality of the soul or as survival on earth through what we have done or through offspring.

We cannot examine here whether or to what extent Christian notions of the Beyond are still alive today. Groethuysen, in his study on the evolving middle class as it emancipates itself from Christian dogmas (1927), stressed very clearly that modern man, while capable of dealing with life, was incapable of dealing with dying. He quotes the pronouncement of a theologian of that period: " 'Woe, how many are there who would gladly forgo Christ's being their savior and would not care about the remedies he offers them for their salvation, were he only to renounce his right to punish them.' This brought it about that God became more and more the specter of death, in that the priests, deprived of their influence, pointed with ever stronger emphasis to death as the wages of sin. The conception began to prevail that a good conscience is the best help for dying; yet death in itself remained alien and contradictory" (p. 128).

Today, in place of generally binding religious notions, such as the Christian notions of Heaven and Hell, uncertainty about the "hereafter" prevails to a great extent—uncertainty and perplexity. In consequence of the belief in *total* death—a belief also championed by modern Protestant theology—the attitude to death has become even more critically sensitive. Bloch (1959) attributes the fact that man is at present apparently able to do without notions of the Beyond, to "previous, satisfying ideals still enduring in his unconscious." "It is due to what has been preserved of them that so-called modern man does not sense that abyss that constantly surrounds him and in the end quite certainly swallows him up. It is due to them that he, quite without intending to, saves his ego-feeling; it is by them that is created the impression that it is not man who 'goes under' but rather that the world one day has the whim no longer to appear to him" (Bloch, 1959, p. 1360).

The uncertainty of the "hereafter" has brought with it a change in man's relationship to his work and to the possibility of accomplishing it within the time span allotted to him. The crucial point today no longer seems to be that one lead a life as free as possible of guilt and offences against religious commands, but rather that the individual, in the arms of a society that will outlast him, attune his life to the norms of that society.

Seen from the viewpoint of history, the death controversy between existential philosophy and dialectical materialism means—with regard to our century—far more than an extraordinary spectacle in which the Marxists denounced existential philosophy for being fascist, and existential philosophers accused the former of having "sacrificed ontological honor" in their dealing with death. Basically, what is revealed in this controversy is the extreme uncertainty of present-day man in his relation to death. The two schools outdo one another in extreme formulations. Despite its temporarily dominating influence on philosophy and theology, existential philosophy has left no lasting imprint on the "public" attitude to death. Dialectical materialism, in its proclamation of "natural" death, in spinning out the bold fantasy of a world that will some day be completely rid of the specter of death, is on the whole in agreement with those forces (for the most part of quite different origin) that have contributed to the repression of death.

Von Ferber to whom we in Germany are indebted for important sociological reflections on the death problem (1970), also stresses the disproportion between the anthropological significance of death and its position in our civilization: "To the extent to which we define death, isolating it, as a problem of medical organization—that is, as a purely private affair—thereby depriving it of its socially crucial role, we destroy the tension between creature existence and social existence from which human freedom arises in the sociohistorical process" (p. 360). Freud's statement (1915a) that "Would it not be better to give death the place in reality and in our thoughts which is its due. . . ." (p. 299)—a statement that is found but once in Freud's work—was written a short time after the first World War. Today, the question arises of the extent to which the events of both world wars, of the concentration camps, of mass destruction, and the use of nuclear weapons and their further development must have affected, and still do affect, our relation to dying and death. They still continue to have an effect. At first glance, the thought comes to mind that the catastrophic events of this century are to be reckoned among the factors causing the repression of death, that it was only by being kept under the wrap of complete silence that the constant confrontation with dying could be borne. This seems to be the more so, since, at the same time, the glorification of dying—the death of a hero—has disappeared, a fact that is evident if we draw a comparison between the First World War and the Second World War. However, the relation between death repression and the great catastrophes of this century can also be seen the other way round. Is it not true that with the repression of death precisely those forces that could have opposed the mass annihilations were paralyzed?

In terms of mortality, therefore, the twentieth century presents an extraordinary picture: outwardly, the repression of death is dominant, and dying and mourning the deceased have become a private matter. Inwardly, dealing with death in his mind, man is split in his relation to death. It seems that the aspects of the fear of death have changed, above all in consequence of the waning of the Christian notions of the Beyond; one cannot, however, infer from this that, today, man has a better chance of living with death. This holds true not only with regard to the vague hopes implicit in the demand for a "natural" death. The possibilities of modern medicine on which these hopes are based, do not, precisely on that point, appear to lead any further.

There is, therefore, still a danger to the individual that he may not find an attitude to death that is adequate to the fact of our mortality, and that he may not escape developing a neurosis based on the problems of death, for society, as well as the individual living within it, tends to sidestep the problems of death. At the beginning of our study, we referred to two attitudes toward the problem of death, the *attention volontaire* and the *attitude spectaculaire passive.* These basic ways of dealing with the problem make it comprehensible that the fear of death—as response to the mortality of man—is capable of affecting him in quite diverse ways. The fear of death may be silenced in favor of man's living only in the present; it may be transformed into multiple anxiety-equivalents and thereby into neurotic symptoms that scarcely betray the original nature of the threat; finally, fear of death may, in exceptional cases, become the sole dominant theme of a neurosis. In all three modes—that is, in repression, in distortion, and in isolated exaggeration, the problems of death become operative in the origin and in the course of neuroses. Under what conditions this influence on the genesis of neuroses is of decisive significance or merely of minor importance—this question cannot at the present time be answered.

References

Adorno, T.W. (1964), *Jargon der Eigentlichkeit* [*Jargon of Authenticity*]. Frankfurt: Suhrkamp.

Aldrich, C. K. (1963), The dying patient's grief. *JAMA*, 184:329-331.

Alexander, I. E. (1961), Studien zur Psychologie des Todes [Studies on the psychology of death]. In: *Perspektiven der Persönlichkeitsforschung*, ed. J. C. Brengelmann and H. P. David. Bern/Stuttgart: Hans Huber, pp. 55-74.

_____ & Adlerstein, A. M. (1958), Affective response to the concept of death in a population of children and early adolescents. In: Fulton, 1965, pp. 111-123.

_____ _____(1959), Death and religion. In: Feifel, 1959b, pp. 271-283.

Anon. (1972), Vorgeschichte und analytische Behandlung eines Patienten mit phobischer Herzneurose [Previous history and analytic treatment of a patient suffering from a phobic cardiac neurosis]. In: *Materialien zur Psychoanalyse.* Göttingen/Zürich: Vandenhoeck & Ruprecht, pp. 45-97.

Anthony, S. (1940), *The Child's Discovery of Death.* London: Kegan Paul, Trench, Trubner.

Bacon, F. (1940), *Essays.* New York: Oxford University Press.

Baelz, E. (1901), Uber Emotionslähmung [On emotional paralysis]. *Allg. Z. Psychiat.*, 58:717-721.

von Baeyer, W., Häfner, H. & Kisker, K. P. (1964), *Psychiatrie der Verfolgten* [*Psychiatry of the Persecuted*]. Berlin/Göttingen/Heidelberg: Springer.

Bally, G. (1964), Die Bedeutung der Angst für die menschliche Verfassung [The significance of anxiety for the human condition]. *Z. Psychother.*, 14:123-139.

_____(1967), Todeserwartung, Sterben und Trauer heute [Expectation of death, dying, and mourning today]. In: *Was weiss man von der Seele?*, ed. H. G. Schultz. Berlin/Stuttgart: Kreuz-Verlag, pp. 94-106.

von Balthasar, H. U. (1956), Der Tod im heutigen Denken [Death in current thought]. *Anima*, 11:292-299.

Barth, K. (1948), *Die kirchliche Dogmatik, III. Bd. Die Lehre von der Schöpfung [Ecclesiastical Dogmatics, Vol. III. The Dogma of Creation]*. Zollikon/Zürich: Evangel. Verlag.

Bauer, A. V. (1971), Der.Tod in Liedern des evangelischen Kirchengesangbuches und in poetischen Texten der Gegenwart [Death in the songs of the Protestant book of hymns, and in poetical texts of the present time]. *Almanach für Literatur und Theologie*, 5. Wuppertal: Hammer-Verlag.

Baumeyer, F. (1954), Der Höhenschwindel [Fear of heights]. *Nervenarzt*, 25:467-473.

Beyme, F. (1963, 1964), Archetypischer Traum (Todeshochzeit) und psychosomatisches Syndrom (weibliche Impotenz) im Lichte der Forschungen von J. J. Bachofen, C. G. Jung und Neumann [An archetypal dream (death nuptials) and a psychosomatic syndrome (female impotency) in the light of investigations by J. J. Bachofen, C. G. Jung, and Neumann]. *Schweiz. Arch. Psychiat.*, 92:140-173 (1963), 93: 100-136 (1964), and 94:137-153 (1964).

Bloch, E. (1959), *Das Prinzip Hoffnung [The Principle of Hope]*. Frankfurt: Suhrkamp.

———(1968), *Atheismus im Christentum [Atheism in Christianity]*. Frankfurt: Suhrkamp.

Boros, L. (1964), *Mysterium mortis*. Olten/Freiburg: Walter.

Bowlby, J. (1960), Separation anxiety. *Internat. J. Psycho-Anal.*, 41:89-113.

Bräutigam, W. (1956), Analyse der hypochondrischen Selbstbeobachtung [Analysis of hypochondriacal self-observation]. *Nervenärzt*, 27:409-418.

———(1964), Typus, Psychodynamik und Psychotherapie herzphobischer Zustände [Type, psychodynamics and psychotherapy of cardiophobic states]. *Z. psychosom. Med.*, 10:276-285.

Bromberg, W. & Schilder, P. (1933), Death and dying. *Psychoanal. Rev.*, 20:133-185.

Brun, R. (1953), Uber Freuds Hypothese vom Todestrieb. [On Freud's hypothesis of the death instinct]. *Psyche*, 7:81-111.

Caprio, F. S. (1950), A study of some psychological reactions during prepubescence to the idea of death. *Psychiat. Quart.*, 24:495-505.

Caruso, J. A. (1952), Bemerkungen über den sogenannten "Todestrieb" [Remarks on the so-called "death instinct"]. *Schweiz. Arch. Psychiat.*, 70:245-258.

_____ (1968), *Die Trennung der Liebenden. Eine Phänomenologie des Todes* [*The Separation of Lovers. A Phenomenology of Death*]. Bern/Stuttgart: Huber.

Chadwick, M. (1929), Notes upon the fear of death. *Internat. J. Psycho-Anal.*, 10:321-334.

Chodoff, P. (1960), A psychiatric approach to the dying patient. *Cancer*, 10:29-32.

Choron, J. (1967), *Der Tod im abendländischen Denken* [*Death in Western Thought*]. Stuttgart: Klett.

Christian, P. & Hahn, P. (1964), Psychosomatische Syndrome im Gefolge internistischer Erkrankungen [Psychosomatic syndromes appearing consequent to internal diseases]. *Internist*, 5:163-171.

Ciompi, L. (1969), Follow-up studies on evolution of former neurotic and depressive states in old age. *J. Geriatric Psychiat.*, 3:90-106.

_____(1972), Allgemeine Psychopathologie des Alterns [General psychopathology of aging]. In: *Psychiatrie der Gegenwart*, II/2. Berlin/Heidelberg/New York: Springer, pp. 1001-1036.

_____ & Müller, C. (1969), Katamnestische Untersuchungen zur Altersentwicklung psychischer Krankheiten [Katamnestic investigations concerning the development of mental illnesses in old age]. *Nervenarzt*, 40:349-355.

Corey, L. C. (1961), An analogue of resistance to death awareness. *J. Gerontol.*, 16:59-60.

Delkeskamp, H. (1965), Langstreckenkatamnesen von Zwangsneurosen [Longitudinal katamneses of obsessional neuroses]. *Acta psychiat. Scand.*, 41:564-581.

Deutsch, H. (1945), *The Psychology of Women*, Vol. 2. New York: Grune & Stratton.

Dichter, E. (1961), *Strategie im Reich der Wünsche* [*Strategy in the Realm of Wishes*]. Düsseldorf: Econ.

Diggory, J. C. & Rothman, D. Z. (1961), Values destroyed by death. In: Fulton, 1965, pp. 152-160.

Edwards, P. (1967), My death. In: *Encyclopedia of Philosophy*, ed. P. Edwards. London: Macmillan, pp. 416-419.

Eissler, K. R. (1955), *The Psychiatrist and the Dying Patient.* New York: International Universities Press.

Eitinger, L. (1969), Anxiety in concentration camp survivors. *Austral. J. Psychiat.*, 3:348-351.

Erikson, E. H. (1954), The dream specimen of psychoanalysis. *J. Amer. Psychoanal. Assn.*, 2:5-56.

Ernst, K. (1959), *Die Prognose der Neurosen* [*The Prognosis of Neuroses*]. Berlin/Göttingen/Heidelberg: Springer.

———— Kind, H. & Rotach-Fuch, M. (1968), *Ergebnisse der Verlaufsforschung bei Neurosen* [*Results of Research on the Course of Neuroses*]. Berlin/Heidelberg/New York: Springer.

Federn, P. (1932), The reality of the death instinct, especially in melancholia. Remarks on Freud's *Civilization and Its Discontents*. *Psychoanal. Rev.*, 19:129-151.

Feifel, H. (1959a), Attitudes towards death in some normal and mentally ill populations. In: Feifel, 1959b, pp. 114-132.

————(1959b), *The Meaning of Death*. New York/Toronto/London: McGraw-Hill.

Feldmann, H. (1967), Situationsanalyse der Zwangsbefürchtung (Phobie) [Situational analysis of obsessional fear (phobia)]. *Arch. Psychiat.*, 209:53-66.

————(1972), *Hypochondrie* [*Hypochondriasis*]. Heidelberg/New York: Springer.

Fenichel, O. (1945), *The Psychoanalytic Theory of Neuroses*. New York: Norton.

von Ferber, C. (1963), Soziologische Aspekte des Todes [Sociological aspects of death]. *Ev. Ethik*, 7:338-360.

————(1970), Der Tod. Ein unbewältigtes Problem für Mediziner und Soziologen [Death. An unmastered problem for physicians and sociologists]. *Kölner Z. Soziologie*, 22:237-250.

Flügel, J. C. (1953), The death instinct, homeostasis and allied concepts. *Internat. J. Psycho-Anal.*, 34:43-74.

Freud, S. (1900), The interpretation of dreams, chapter 5. *Standard Edition*, 4:163-276. London: Hogarth Press, 1953.

————(1913a), Totem and taboo. *Standard Edition*, 13:1-161. London: Hogarth Press, 1955.

————(1913b), The theme of the three caskets. *Standard Edition*, 12:291-301. London: Hogarth Press, 1958.

————(1915a), Thoughts for the times on war and death. *Standard Edition*, 14:274-300. London: Hogarth Press, 1957.

————(1915b), The unconscious. *Standard Edition*, 14:151-216. London: Hogarth Press, 1957.

————(1916), Some character types met with in psychoanalytic work. *Standard Edition*, 14:311-333. London: Hogarth Press, 1957.

————(1917), Anxiety. In: Introductory lectures on psycho-analysis. *Standard Edition*, 16:392-411. London: Hogarth Press, 1963.

————(1920), Beyónd the pleasure principle. *Standard Edition*, 18:7-64. London: Hogarth Press, 1955.

_____(1923), The ego and the id. *Standard Edition*, 19:3-66. London: Hogarth Press, 1961.

_____(1926), Inhibitions, symptoms and anxiety. *Standard Edition*, 20:87-172. London: Hogarth Press, 1959.

_____ (1933), Anxiety and instinctual life. In: New introductory lectures on psychoanalysis. *Standard Edition*, 22:81-111. London: Hogarth Press, 1964.

Friedman, D. B. (1961), Death anxiety and the primal scene. *Psychoanal. Rev.*, 48:108-118.

Fromm, E. (1951), *The Forgotten Language: An Introduction to the Understanding of Dreams, Fairy Tales and Myths.* New York: Rinehart.

Fuchs, W. (1969), *Todesbilder in der modernen Gesellschaft* [*Images of Death in Modern Society*]. Frankfurt: Suhrkamp.

Fulton, R., ed. (1965), *Death and Identity.* New York/London/ Sidney: Wiley.

Gardner, R. A. (1969), The guilt reaction of parents of children with severe physical disease. *Amer. J. Psychiat.*, 126:636-644.

von Gebsattel, V. E. (1938), Die Welt des Zwangskranken [The world of the obsessional patient]. *Moschr. Psychiat.*, 99: 10-74.

_____(1948), Zur Psychopathologie der Sucht [On the psychopathology of addiction]. *Stud. Generale*, 1:258-265.

_____(1951), Anthropologie der Angst [Anthropology of anxiety]. *Hochland*, 43:352-364.

_____(1954), Aspekte des Todes [Aspects of death]. In *Prolegomena einer medizinischen Anthropologie.* Berlin/Göttingen/Heidelberg: Springer, pp. 389-412.

_____(1959), Die phobische Fehlhaltung [The phobic attitude]. In: *Handb. der Neurosenlehre*, 2:102-124. Munich/Berlin: Urban & Schwarzenberg.

Gehlen, A. (1962), *Der Mensch [Man]*. Frankfurt/Bonn: Athenäum.

Gesell, A. (1946), *The Child from Five to Ten.* New York: Harper Brothers.

Glaser, B. G. & Strauss, A. L. (1965), *Awareness of Dying.* Chicago: Aldine.

Gollwitzer, H. (1971), Exkurs über das Todesproblem im Marxismus [A discourse on the problem of death in Marxism]. *Almanach für Literatur und Theologie*, 5:49-56.

Göppert, H. (1964), Zwang und Zwangsneurose [Obsession and obsessional neurosis]. *Zeitschr. f. Psychother.*, 14:87-95.

Gorer, G. (1965), *Death, Grief and Mourning in Contemporary Britain*. London: Cresset Press.

Gössling, S. (n.d.), Der Tod ein ständiger Gast [Death—a permanent guest]. Unpublished.

Groetuysen, B. (1927), *Die Entstehung der bürgerlichen Welt- und Lebensanschauung in Frankreich* [*The Formation of the Bourgeois* Weltanschauung *and Philosophy of Life in France*]. Halle: Niemeyer.

Grotjahn, M. (1951), About the representation of death in the art of antiquity and in the unconscious of men. In: *Psychoanalysis and Culture*, ed. G. B. Wilbur & W. Muensterberger. New York: International Universities Press, pp. 410-424.

Guardini, R. (1953), *Die Lebensalter. Ihre ethische und pädagogische Bedeutung* [*Man's Ages. Their Ethical and Pedagogical Significance*]. Würzburg: Werkbund Verlag.

_____(1961), *Rainer Maria Rilkes Deutung des Daseins* [*Rainer Maria Rilke's Interpretation of Existence*]. Munich: Kösel.

Hall, G. S. (1915), Thanatophobia and immortality. *Amer. J. Psychol.*, 26:550-613.

_____(1922), *Senescence*. New York: Appleton.

Handal, P. I. & Rychlack, J. F. (1971), Curvilinearity between dream content and death anxiety and the relationship of death anxiety to repression sensitization. *J. Abnorm. Psychol.*, 77:11-16.

Heidegger, M. (1927), *Sein und Zeit* [*Being and Time*]. Halle: Niemeyer.

Herzog, E. (1960), *Psyche und Tod* [*Psyche and Death*]. Zürich: Stuttgart: Rascher.

Heveroch, A. (1914), Woher stammt unser Seins-Bewusstsein? [How did our consciousness of Being come about?] *Arch. Psychiat.*, 53:593-648.

Hoffman, F. H. & Brody, M. W. (1957), The symptom, fear of death. *Psychoanal. Rev.*, 44:433-438.

Horkheimer, M. & Adorno, T. W. (1969), *Dialektik der Aufklärung* [*Dialectics of Enlightenment*]. Frankfurt: Fischer.

Hutschnecker, A. A. (1959), Personality factors in dying patients. In: Feifel, 1959b, pp. 237-250.

Huxley, A. (1959), Drugs that shape men's minds. In: *Collected Essays*. New York: Harper, pp. 336-340.

Janzarik, W. (1965), Psychologie und Psychopathologie der Zukunftsbezogenheit [Psychology and psychopathology of living in terms of the future]. *Arch. Ges. Psychol.*, 117:33-53.

Jaques, E. (1965), Death and the mid-life crisis. *Internat. J. Psycho-Anal.*, 46:502-514.

Jaspers, K. (1965), *Philosophie II*. Berlin/Göttingen/Heidelberg: Springer.

Jeffers, F. C., Nichols, C. R. & Eisdorfer, C. (1961), Attitudes of older persons toward death: A preliminary study. *J. Gerontol.*, 16:53-56.

Jung, C. G. (1947), Seele und Tod [Soul and death]. In: *Wirklichkeit der Seele*. Zürich: Rascher, pp. 212-230.

Jüngel, E. (1971), *Tod* [*Death*]. Stuttgart/Berlin: Kreuz-Verlag.

Kastenbaum, R. (1959), Time and death in adolescence. In: Feifel, 1959b, pp. 99-113.

_____ (1965), The realm of death: An emerging area in psychological research. *J. Human Rev.*, 13:538-551.

Keiser, S. (1952), Body ego during orgasm. *Psychoanal. Quart.*, 21:153-171.

Kemper, W. (1955), *Der Traum und seine Be-Deutung* [*The Dream and its Interpretation/Meaning*]. Hamburg: Rowohlt.

Kierkegaard, S. (1957), *Die Krankheit zum Tode* [*The Sickness unto Death*]. Düsseldorf: E. Diederich.

Klein, M. (1948), A contribution to the theory of anxiety and guilt. *Internat. J. Psycho-Anal.*, 29:114-123.

_____ (1955), On identification. In: *New Directions in Psycho-Analysis*, ed. M. Klein, P. Heimann, & R. E. Money-Kyrle. New York: Basic Books, pp. 309-345.

Kral, V. A. (1951), Psychiatric observations under severe chronic stress. *Amer. J. Psychiat.*, 108:185-192.

_____ & Gold, S. (1961), Psychiatric findings in a geriatric outpatient clinic. *Canad. Med. Assn. J.*, 84:588-590.

Kübler-Ross, E. (1969), *On Death and Dying*. London: Macmillan.

Kulenkampf, C. & Bauer, A. (1960), Uber das Syndrom der Herzphobie [On the syndrome of cardiac phobia]. *Nervenarzt*, 31:443-454, 496-507.

_____ _____(1962), Herzphobie und Herzinfarkt [Cardiac phobia and cardiac infarction]. *Nervenarzt*, 33:289-299.

Landsberg, P. L. (1937), Die Erfahrung des Todes [The experience of death]. Luzern: Vita nova.

Leroy, E. (1926), *Les visions du demi-sommeil* [*The Visions of Half-sleep*]. Paris: F. Alcan.

Lester, D. (1967), Experimental and correlational studies of the fear of death. *Psychol. Bull.*, 67:27-36.

Lévy-Bruhl, L. (1926), *Das Denken der Naturvölker* [*The Think-ing of Primitive Peoples*]. Wien/Leipzig: Braumüller.
Lieberman, M. A. & Coplan, A. S. (1970), Distance from death as a variable in the study of aging. *Developmental Psychol.*, 2:71-84.
Loeser, L. H. & Bry, T. (1960), The role of death fears in the etiology of phobic anxiety as revealed in group psycho-therapy. *Internat. J. Group Psychother.*, 10:287-297.
Marcuse, H. (1959), The ideology of death. In: Feifel, 1959b, pp. 64-78.
———(1968), *Triebstruktur und Gesellschaft* [*The Structure of Instincts and the Society*]. Frankfurt: Suhrkamp.
Marks, J. M. (1969), *Fears and Phobias*. London: Heinemann.
Marti, K. (1969), *Leichenreden* [*Funeral Orations*]. Neuwied/Berlin: Luchterhand.
Matussek, P. (1948), *Metaphysische Probleme der Medizin* [*Metaphysical Problems of Medicine*]. Berlin/Heidelberg: Springer.
——— (1952), Zur Psychodynamik des Glücksspielers [On the psychodynamics of the gambler]. *Jb. Psychol. u. Psycho-ther.*, 1:232-252.
——— (1959), Süchtige Fehlhaltungen [Failures due to addic-tion]. In: *Hb. Neurosenlehre Psychotherap.*, 118-212. Mu-nich/Berlin: Urban Schwarzenberg.
Metzger, A. (1955), *Freiheit und Tod* [*Freedom and Death*]. Tübingen: Niemeyer.
Meyer, J. E. (1957), Depersonalisation und Zwang als polare Störungen der Ich-Aussenwelt Beziehung [Depersonaliza-tion and obsession as polar disturbances of the ego-ex-ternal world relation]. *Psychiatria et Neurologia*, 133:63-79.
———(1959), *Die Entfremdungserlebnisse* [*Experiences of Alien-ation*]. Stuttgart: Thieme.
———(1961a), Die abnormen Erlebnisreaktionen im Kriege [Ab-normal reactions to war experiences]. In: *Psychiatrie der Gegenwart III*, ed. H. W. Gruhle et al. Berlin/Göt-tingen/Heidelberg: Springer.
———(1961b), Konzentrative Entspannungsübungen nach Elsa Gindler und ihre Grundlagen [Relaxation therapy accord-ing to Elsa Gindler, and its bases]. *Z. Psychother.*, 11:116-127.
Middleton, W. C. (1936/37), Some reactions toward death among college students. *J. Abnorm. Soc. Psychol.*, 31:165-173.

Minkowski, E. (1971), *Die gelebte Zeit* [*The Time That Has Been Lived*]. Salzburg: Müller.

Mitscherlich, A. (1961/62), Anmerkungen über die Chronifizierung psychosomatischen Geschehens [Remarks on the chronification of psychosomatic processes]. *Psyche*, 15: 1-25.

———(1974), Psychoneuroses and neurotic reactions in old age. *J. Amer. Geriat. Soc.*, 22:254-257.

——— & Mitscherlich-Nielsen, M. (1967), *Die Unfähigkeit zu trauern* [*The Inability to Mourn*]. Munich: H. Piper.

Money-Kyrle, R. E. (1955), An inconsclusive contribution to the theory of the death instinct. In: *New Directions in Psycho-Analysis*, ed. M. Klein, P. Heimann, & R. E. Money-Kyrle. London: Tavistock Publications, pp. 499-509.

Moore, D. C., Holton, C. P. & Marten, G. W. (1969), Psychological problems in the management of adolescents with malignancy. *Clin. Ped.*, 8:464-473.

Muensterberger, W. (1963), Vom Ursprung des Todes [The origin of death]. *Psyche*, 17:169-185.

Müller, C. (1957), Weitere Beobachtungen zum Verlauf der Zwangskrankheit [Further observations on the course of obsessional disease]. *Psychiat. Neurol.*, 133:80-94.

Munnichs, J. M. A. (1968), Die Einstellung zur Endlichkeit und zum Tod [The attitude toward finiteness and toward death]. In: *Altern*, ed. H. Thomae & U. Lehr. Frankfurt: Akad. Verlagsges, pp. 579-612.

Nagy, M. N. (1959), The child's view of death. In: Feifel., 1959b, pp. 79-98.

Norton, J. (1968), Die Behandlung einer sterbenden Patientin [The treatment of a dying female patient]. *Psyche*, 22: 98-117.

Ohlmeier, D. & Radebold, H. (1972), Ubertragungs—und Abwehrprozesse in der Initialphase einer Gruppenanalyse mit Patienten im höheren Lebensalter [Processes of transference and of defense in the initial phase of a group therapy with patients of advanced age]. *Gruppenpsychother. und Gruppendynamik*, 5:289-302.

van Oyen, H. (1963), Aufklärungs—und Schweigepflicht des Arztes aus der Sicht der Ethik [The physician's duty to inform and to be silent, seen from the viewpoint of ethics]. *Wege zum Menschen*, 15:385-393.

Peller, L. (1963), Further comments on adoption. *Bull. Phil. Assn. Psychoanal.*, 13:1-13.

Petrilowitsch, N. (1964), *Probleme der Psychotherapie alternder Menschen* [*Problems of Psychotherapy with Aging Persons*]. Basel/New York: Karger.

Pflanz, M. (1962), *Sozialer Wandel und Krankheit* [*Social Change and Illness*]. Stuttgart: Enke.

Plessner, H. (1951), Uber die Beziehung der Zeit zum Tode [On the relation of time to death]. *Eranos Jb.*, 20:349-386.

Plügge, H. (1962), *Wohlbefinden und Missbefinden* [*Feeling Well and Feeling Ill*]. Tübingen: Niemeyer.

Pollock, K. & Kastenbaum, R. (1964), Delay of gratification in later life. In: *New Thoughts on Old Age*, ed. R. Kastenbaum. New York: Springer, pp. 281-290.

De Quincey, T. (1966), *Confessions of an English Opium Eater*. New York: New American Lib.

Rado, S. (1933), The psychoanalysis of a pharmacothymia. *Psychoanal. Quart.*, 2:1-23.

———(1957), Narcotic bondage. In: *Problems of Addiction and and Habituation*, ed. P. H. Hoch & J. Zubin. New York/London: Grune & Stratton, 1958, pp. 27-36.

Rehm, W. (1928), *Der Todesgedanke in der deutschen Dichtung vom Mittelalter bis zur Romantik* [*The Motif of Death in German Poetry from the Middle Ages to the Period of Romanticism*]. Halle: Niemeyer.

Reichard, S., Livson, F. & Peterson, P. G. (1962), *Aging and Personality*. New York: Wiley.

Rheingold, J. C. (1967), *The Mother, Anxiety and Death*. Boston: Little Brown.

Rhudick, P. J. & Dibner, A. S. (1961), Age, personality, and health correlates of death concerns in normal aged individuals. *J. Geront.*, 16:44-49.

Richter, H. E. & Beckmann, D. (1969), *Herzneurose* [*Cardiac Neurosis*]. Stuttgart: Thieme.

Riemann, F. (1967), Die Bedeutung der Angst im menschlichen Leben [The importance of anxiety in human life]. In: *Was weiss man von der Seele?*, ed H. J. Schultz. Berlin/Stuttgart: Kreuz-Verlag, pp. 84-93.

———(1969), *Grundformen der Angst* [*Basic Forms of Anxiety*]. Munich/Basel: Reinhardt.

Riviere, J. (1932), The unconscious phantasy of an inner world reflected in examples from English literature. *Internat. J. Psycho-Anal.*, 11:160-172.

Rosenzweig, F. (1954), *Der Stern der Erlösung* [*The Star of Deliverance*]. Heidelberg: Lambert Schneider.

Roth, M. (1960), The phobic anxiety-depersonalization syndrome and some general aetiological problems in psychiatry. *J. Neuropsychiat.*, 1:293-306.

Sarnoff, I. & Corwin, S. M. (1959), Castration anxiety and the fear of death. *J. Person.*, 27:374-385.

Sartre, J. P. (1952), *Das Sein und das Nichts [Being and Nothingness].* Hamburg: Rowohlt.

Scheler, M. (1933), Tod und Fortleben [Death and continuing to exist]. In: *Zur Ethik und Erkenntnislehre.* Berlin: Der Neue Geist Verlag.

Schilder, P. & Wechsler, D. (1934), The attitudes of children toward death. *J. Genetic Psychol.*, 45:406-451.

Schmidt, G. (1970), Der Todestrieb bei Heinrich von Kleist [The death instinct in Heinrich v. Kleist]. *Munch. Med. Moschr.* 112:758-763.

Schulte, W. (1962), Das Altern als Indikationsfeld für den Therapeuten [Aging as a field of indications for the psychotherapist]. *Wege zum Menschen*, 14:87-96.

Schwidder, W. (1959), Angst und Neurosestruktur [Anxiety and the structure of neurosis]. *Z. Psychosomat. Med.*, 6:91-100.

———(1972), Klinik der Neurosen [The clinical syndromes of neuroses]. In: *Psychiatrie der Gegenwart.* Berlin/Heidelberg/New York: Springer, pp. 341-346.

Shepherd, M., Cooper, B., Brown, A. C. & Kalton, G. (1966), *Psychiatric Illness in General Practice.* London: University Press.

Simmel, E. (1944), Self-preservation and the death instinct. *Psychoanal. Quart.*, 13:160-185.

Simmel, G. (1918), *Lebensanschauung [View of Life].* Munich/Leipzig: Duncker & Humbolt, pp. 106-132.

Skoog, G. (1965), Onset of anancastic conditions. *Acta psychiat. Scand. Suppl.*, 184. Copenhagen: Munksgaard.

Slater, P. E. (1964), Prolegomena to a psychoanalytic theory of aging and death. In: *New Thoughts on Old Age*, ed. R. Kastenbaum. New York: Springer, pp. 19-40.

Spiegelberg, U. & Betz, B. (1969), Neurose im Alter [Neurosis in old age]. *Arch. Psychiat.*, 212:294-308.

Stekel, W. (1922), *Conditions of Nervous Anxiety and Their Treatment.* London: Kegan Paul.

Stern, K., Williams, G. M. & Prados, M. (1951), Grief reactions in later life. *Amer. J. Psychiat.*, 58:289-294.

Stern, M. M. (1972), Trauma, death anxiety and fear of death. *Psyche*, 26:901-928.

Stork, J. (1972), Suizidtendenz und Suizidversuch. Statistische Analyse des suizidalen Feldes bei Schülern [Suicidal tendencies and attempts to commit suicide. Statistical analysis of the field of suicide among pupils]. *Z. klin. Psychol. & Psychother.*, 20:123-151.

Straus, E. (1930), *Geschehnis und Erlebnis* [*Event and Experience*]. Berlin: J. Springer.

⎯⎯⎯⎯⎯(1938), Ein Beitrag zur Psychologie der Zwangserscheinungen [A contribution to the psychology of obsessional symptoms]. *Moschr. Psychiatr. Neurol.*, 98:61-101.

⎯⎯⎯⎯⎯ (1949), Die Asthesiologie und ihre Bedeutung für das Verständnis der Halluzinationen [Aesthesiology and its significance for the understanding of hallucinations]. *Arch. Psychiat.*, 182:301-332.

Swenson, W. M. (1961), Attitudes towards death in an aged population. *J. Gerontol.*, 16:49-52.

⎯⎯⎯⎯⎯(1965), Attitudes towards death among the aged. In: Fulton, 1965, pp. 105-110.

Teicher, J. D. (1965), "Combat fatigue" or death anxiety neurosis. In: Fulton, 1965, pp. 249-258.

von Tepl, Johannes (1967), *Der Ackermann aus Böhmen* [*The Husbandman from Bohemia*]. Reclam (nr. 7666): Stuttgart.

Tillich, P. (1959), The eternal now. In: Feifel, 1959b, pp. 30-38.

⎯⎯⎯⎯⎯(1969), *Sein und Sinn* [*Being and Meaning*]. Ev. Werke XI. Stuttgart: Ev. Verlagswerk.

Trillhaas, W. (1965), Einige Bemerkungen zur Idee der Unsterblichkeit [Some comments on the idea of immortality]. *Neue Z. system. Theologie*, 7:143-160.

Wahl, C. W. (1958), The fear of death. In: Fulton, 1965, pp. 56-66.

Weisman, A. D. & Hackett, T. P. (1965), Predilection to death. In: Fulton, 1965, pp. 293-332.

Williams, M. (1966), Changing attitudes to death. *Human Relations*, 18:405-423.

Winnicott, D. W. (1965), *The Maturational Processes and the Facilitating Environment.* New York: International Universities Press.

Wyss, D. (1968), *Strukturen der Moral* [*Structures of Morals*]. Göttingen: Vandenhoeck & Ruprecht.

Yourcenar, M. (1951), *Memoirs of Hadrian.* New York: Farrar Strauss, 1963.